Simon & Schuster
New York   London   Toronto   Sydney   New Delhi

Lessons from

MADAME

CHIC

20 Stylish Secrets
I Learned
While Living in Paris

JENNIFER L. SCOTT

Simon & Schuster
1230 Avenue of the Americas
New York, NY 10020

This Simon & Schuster hardcover edition November 2012

SIMON & SCHUSTER and colophon are registered trademarks of Simon & Schuster, Inc.

For information about special discounts for bulk purchases, please contact Simon & Schuster Special Sales at 1-866-506-1949 or business@simonandschuster.com.

The Simon & Schuster Speakers Bureau can bring authors to your live event. For more information or to book an event contact the Simon & Schuster Speakers Bureau at 1-866-248-3049 or visit our website at www.simonspeakers.com.

Designed by Nancy Singer

Illustrations by Virginia Johnson

Manufactured in the United States of America

10 9 8 7

Library of Congress Cataloging-in-Publication Data
Scott, Jennifer L. (Jennifer Lynn)
  Lessons from Madame Chic : 20 stylish secrets I learned while living in Paris / Jennifer L. Scott.
    p.   cm.
  1. Charm. 2. Fashion. 3. Home economics. 4. Women—France—Paris—Social life and customs. 5. French—Social life and customs. 6. Paris (France)—Social life and customs. 7. Paris (France)—Civilization. I. Title.
BJ1610.S395 2012
646.7'6—dc23
2012017494

ISBN 978-1-4516-9937-1
ISBN 978-1-4767-0279-7 (ebook)

For Arabella and Georgina

Contents

CONTENTS

Part 2
STYLE AND BEAUTY

Part 3
HOW TO LIVE WELL

Contents

Introduction

I relax in the upholstered living room armchair. The smell of tobacco lingers in the air. The grand windows are open, allowing the warm Parisian night breeze to flow through the room, and the exquisite tapestry drapes end in an elegant puddle on the floor. Classical music plays on the vintage record player. The dishes are nearly cleared away but the last coffee cups still remain on the dining room table, along with a few crumbs of that day's fresh baguette, so eagerly consumed earlier with a slice of Camembert cheese—the *roi du fromage*.

Monsieur Chic sits smoking his pipe in tranquil contemplation while nodding his head slowly to the music as though conducting the orchestra in his imagination. His son paces by the open window, holding a glass of port. Madame Chic walks in, removing the apron that so efficiently protected her A-line skirt and silk blouse. She smiles contentedly, and I help her remove the final coffee cups from the table. It has been another satisfying day in Paris—where life is lived beautifully, passionately.

In January 2001 I went to live with a French family in Paris as a foreign exchange student. I left the casual comforts of Los Angeles, boarded a plane with my fellow students from the University of Southern California (with two very large, overstuffed suitcases), and embarked on an adventure that would alter the course of my life in the most profound ways.

But, of course, I didn't know that then. All I knew was that I was going to spend the next six months in Paris. *Paris!* The most romantic city in the world! I confess my excitement was clouded by some concerns. When I left California, I had only taken three semesters of French—my command of the language was clumsy at best. Also, six months is a long time to be away from one's family and country. What if I got homesick? What would my French host family be like? Would I like them? Would they like me?

So a few nights after I landed in Paris, when I found myself sitting in the formal and austere dining room of Famille Chic, partaking in a five-course dinner, surrounded by floor-to-ceiling windows and precious antiques, I was already in love with my new, fascinating family. This family who was beautifully dressed, eating a well-cooked homemade meal (in courses!) on their best china on a Wednesday evening. This family who took tremendous enjoyment from the small pleasures in life and who appeared to have mastered the art of living well. This family with their nightly rituals and immaculate customs, built on tradition.

How could this simple California girl, who was so accustomed to flip-flops and barbecues, have found herself living amongst the Parisian aristocracy?

Yes, Famille Chic (the name I will use to preserve their anonymity) were of an aristocratic heritage. Their tradition of fine living had been passed down to them from their illustrious ancestors, and generations upon generations of Famille Chic had practiced their art.

And who was this enigmatic Madame Chic? She was a mother and a wife. She worked part-time and volunteered. She was very traditional in her style; she never wore jeans. She was a brunette with a no-nonsense Parisian bob. She had very strong opinions. She was kind and nurturing and she could be bold and blunt (as you will see). She was a woman who knew what was important in life, and her family was the most important thing of all. She was the head of this household that lived so well. She made all of those delectable meals. She managed the intricacies of everyday life. She steered the ship.

In the beginning of my stay I thought all French families lived like Famille Chic—in a traditional and ceremonious manner. Then I had the pleasure of getting to know Famille Bohemienne (another host family in my study abroad program). Their household was run by Madame Bohemienne, a single mother with curly hair, a rosy outlook on life, and warmth and charm that illuminated her wild dinner parties. In contrast to Famille

Chic, the Bohemiennes were casual, relaxed, boisterous, and well, bohemian! Yes, the two families lived their lives very differently, but both families lived passionate lives and lived them very well. It was my pleasure and privilege to observe them both.

This book originated on my blog, *The Daily Connoisseur*, when I did a series called *The Top 20 Things I Learned While Living in Paris*. I received so much interest from readers, I decided to elaborate on the lessons I learned from Famille Chic and Famille Bohemienne and record them in this book.

Each chapter presents a lesson I learned while living in Paris. Many of these lessons were learned directly from Madame Chic, whom I had the pleasure of observing in her own home and who so kindly took me under her wing. I learned some of the lessons from Madame Bohemienne. Some lessons I learned from the City of Light itself.

As a young college student, I had many ideas about what I'd learn while living in Paris, but I didn't expect to learn so much about how to live life. How to *really* live it. How not just to exist, but to thrive. Ah, but I am getting ahead of myself . . .

Lessons from

MADAME
CHIC

Part 1

DIET AND
EXERCISE

Chapter 1

SNACKING IS SO NOT CHIC

When living with a different family (especially in a foreign country), one finds many causes for anxiety. One cause, for me, was food. Back home in California I was used to grazing all day long. A handful of crackers here, an orange there, some cookies here, a yogurt there . . . Would I feel comfortable going into Famille Chic's kitchen and foraging as if I were in my own home?

A few hours after my first dinner with Famille Chic, I began to feel hungry. I had had a delicious dinner, but being slightly nervous around my new host family, and feeling anxious about conducting an entire conversation based on three semesters of college French, I hadn't eaten as much as I would have liked. So I thought I'd tiptoe (in my pajamas) to the kitchen, which I had, up until then, yet to visit.

Famille Chic's kitchen was not easily accessible. It was at the back of the apartment, down a long, dark hallway, and was not attached to any other room. I thought I'd sneak down the hall and have a peek. Perhaps there was a bowl of fruit for me to nibble on.

Of course the door to my room (being as ancient and fabulous as it was) let out a grandiloquent squeak as I began my stealth mission, and after a few moments, Madame Chic was down the hallway in her dressing gown, asking if I was okay. I assured her I was and that I was simply going to get a glass of water. She said she'd get one for me. And apart from the strange look she gave my pajamas (which I will address in another chapter), everything seemed to be okay. Except it wasn't. I wanted my midnight snack!

I went to bed that night slightly hungry, a sensation I was not accustomed to. The feeling wasn't that bad; in fact, it intrigued me! I had never allowed myself to get hungry. In California I would find something to eat at the first sign of hunger pangs, completely eliminating the feeling as soon as possible. That night I relished my hunger and had fantasies about what would be for breakfast the next day.

It did take me a while to catch on, but I finally realized that most French people do not snack—and Famille Chic was no exception. The entire six months I lived with them, I never saw a single member of their household eat anything outside allotted mealtimes. They had excellent eating habits, were not overweight in the slightest, and gastronomically speaking, led very balanced lives.

I never saw Monsieur Chic rushing out of the house with an apple in his mouth and a takeaway coffee in his hand because he was running late for work. Every morning the family would have breakfast at the same time (and breakfast was a very satisfying meal), then lunch would usually be eaten outside the home, presumably sitting down in a café, and dinner was always at least a three-course sit-down affair at home. If you had that to look forward to every day, you wouldn't ruin your appetite by stuffing yourself with crackers either!

Le No-Snacking Design

Many modern American homes boast an open-plan kitchen, where the cooking, dining, and living spaces all seamlessly flow together in one giant room. This kind of interior is not common in Paris's ancient apartments. The journey to Famille Chic's kitchen was a small trek. Not only was the kitchen not attached to any room (certainly not the dining room), but it was situated at the end of a long, dark corridor that usually had washing hanging in it. You might argue that having an open-plan kitchen is warmer and more welcoming (after all, the kitchen is the heart of the home), but it also presents temptations. It is terribly difficult to avoid the cookie jar if it is staring you in the face while you try to mind your own business in the living room.

Famille Chic's kitchen was purely functional. While many modern kitchens boast granite countertops, stainless steel appliances, and espresso makers, Famille Chic's kitchen was tiny and quite dated. Its main function was to turn out meals (albeit spectacular meals). Breakfast was the only meal of the day consumed in the kitchen; dinner was always served in the dining room.

Famille Chic's living room was very formal. It was not the sort of place one would lounge in while snacking. There was no comfy sectional with throw pillows, no La-Z-Boy chair, no giant flat-screen TV. Instead, there were four antique armchairs. They did have a tiny, dated television, which they rarely watched—but it was tucked away in the corner. Famille Chic's living room was set up for conversation, entertaining, or reading a book. And because it was so formal, one would have felt quite strange devouring cheese puffs out of the bag whilst in it.

Snacking is not chic. Have you ever watched someone mindlessly snacking? Sitting in front of the television with a bag of pretzels or a pint of ice cream—absentmindedly eating while not really paying attention? Perhaps crumbs are falling down the front of his shirt. Or an errant drop of ice cream ruins her freshly pressed skirt. Snacking is the opposite of chic. And in Paris, that simply won't do.

High-Quality Snacking

Back home, I admit that I will snack, but only if it's a high-quality snack. Before living in France, I would think nothing of eating really poor-quality foods like drugstore candy, potato chips out of the bag, or crackers out of the box. Now I avoid eating these things at all costs. My snack foods must be high quality—Greek yogurt with blueberries, a bowl of tomato soup, or a piece of fruit. And I have definitely eliminated the midnight junk food snack I used to have. My husband and I have dinner quite early now that we have children, and I no longer need anything after dinner. I find that if I have a well-balanced, quality dinner and a small dessert, the need for a snack is completely eliminated.

I suggest that you do not even bring low-quality snack foods into your home. Don't even go down that aisle in the grocery store. If it isn't readily available, you won't miss it after a while. I promise you will not think back fondly about those addictive cheesy powdered crackers. Instead, you'll wonder how you could ever have consumed such a horrid thing in the first place.

Never Eat on the Go

The French do not eat while on the run. In the book *Sixty Million Frenchmen Can't Be Wrong*, authors Jean-Benoît Nadeau and Julie Barlow recall walking out of their apartment building in Paris while simultaneously eating a sandwich and being met with a sarcastic *"Bon appétit"* from the sneering doorman. The only people you see eating and walking at the same time in France are tourists. I can't even imagine Madame Chic doing such a thing—it just would *never* happen!

I used to think nothing of eating and walking at the same time. Now I would rather not, *merci*. In fact the other day I was out shopping and realized I was quite hungry. I briefly considered stopping in one of those pretzel places and getting a giant pretzel to eat while I shopped, but when I imagined Madame Chic's disapproving glance, I simply could not bring myself to do it. I opted, instead, to walk to the food court, sit down, and eat my lunch like a lady.

Eating should command your full attention. After all, you are bringing things into your body. The act should be civilized and respectful. This cannot be achieved on the subway. If you must snack, do so in a controlled and civilized manner. Pop into a café and have a seat to enjoy your cappuccino and croissant.

Allow Yourself to Feel Hungry

So many of us snack because we don't want to feel hungry. I learned in France that feeling hungry is a very good thing. You're not starving. You have an appetite, which is the result of lots of stimulating activity.

My days in Paris were extremely active. I was out all day long, walking in the city, going to classes, meeting with friends. I built up a tremendous appetite! And that marvelous appetite would be satisfied every evening when I came home and dined with Famille Chic. I was able to appreciate Madame Chic's well-cooked meals and really savor them. If I had spoilt my appetite by indulging in crackers or candy beforehand, I wouldn't have appreciated her meals at all. Who wants to ruin sole with beurre blanc, new potatoes, and haricots verts, followed by a crème caramel, by eating too much bread before dinner? Not me!

Diagnose the Problem

Many times what we think is hunger is actually something else. If you are eating three balanced meals a day and afternoon tea, you probably aren't hungry. You might be feeling thirst or acute dehydration. The next time you feel like snacking between meals, have a tall glass of water with lemon instead and wait twenty minutes. Chances are your hunger will dissipate.

If you are not thirsty and you have a feeling you are not really hungry, could you be bored? Most of us have snacked out of boredom at some point in our lives. Amuse yourself with other pursuits—reading a book, getting some fresh air on a walk, or playing the piano . . .

And finally, try not to snack in front of the TV, unless you are watching the Super Bowl.

Make Dining Well a Priority

Of course, all this effort to not snack is futile if you are not eating at least three balanced meals a day. Do you feel like you can never get ahead when it comes to planning meals? Are you always wondering where your next meal will come from? (Take out? Delivery? Rummaging around the kitchen cabinets?) Are you slightly neurotic when it comes to food? Maybe snacks are taking the place of meals in your life.

Famille Chic made meals a priority and enjoyed them ritualistically. There was not one night where we considered ordering pizza delivery because there was nothing for dinner. Or, even worse, stood above the kitchen sink while eating a bowl of cereal at nine p.m. because dinner failed to happen. (We've all been there—especially me. I'm not denying it!)

Madame Chic had a set of recipes that she made very well, and she provided them in rotation. The pantry was always stocked with the ingredients to make a satisfying meal. On the nights when we didn't have a spectacular casserole or some other delight, we would have salad with select cuts of cured meats from the charcuterie. Even this dinner held importance, and the tray of cured meats (salamis, sopressatas, etc.) was passed around the table as though it held the most exquisite delicacies.

Every day they enjoyed real food (no fake butter, fake sugar, or diet anything). Their meals were rich, decadent, and very traditionally French.

 Le Recap

- Boost the quality of the meals you do have to reduce the craving for snack foods.

- Make dining well a priority.

- Decorate your home for not snacking. Go for aesthetics first and comfort second. (After all, if you feel like lying down, you can always go to bed.)

- When you do snack, pick only high-quality foods. Never settle.

- Never eat while walking, driving, or standing. Avoid eating on the go at all costs.

- Allow yourself to feel a little bit of hunger to build up a healthy appetite.

- Stay hydrated throughout the day with water.

- Always consult your doctor before starting any new eating routine and work out what is best for you.

- Make preparing balanced meals a priority in your life and keep your pantry stocked.

- And remember: mindless snacking is so not chic!

Chapter 2

DEPRIVE YOURSELF NOT

have never consistently eaten better, nor enjoyed my food more, than when I lived in Paris with Famille Chic. This was a family who, gastronomically speaking, led a rather enviable existence.

Breakfast consisted of toasted *tartines* with real butter and homemade jam, among other delights. Lunch was either taken outside the home or, if inside the home, often consisted of leftovers from the previous evening. Occasionally Madame Chic would have her girlfriends over for lunch, in which case she would make something light like fish and steamed vegetables with a delicate sauce, or a quiche and salad. Dinner was at least a three-course affair every evening. A typical weeknight meal would be something like leek soup, followed by roast chicken with braised endive and new potatoes, followed by a salad, followed by a strawberry tart and finally the cheese course. Dinner was most often a French meal; Madame Chic did not experiment with other cuisines. There was always a protein (usually chicken, eggs, fish, or beef), vegetables, and rich sauces. Cheese was offered every night—as was dessert!

As an American, and specifically a Southern Californian, I was initially a bit hesitant when confronted with these decadent meals. Was I going to become fat while living in France? I had hoped to return home to my friends and family chic and mysterious—perhaps with a new haircut à la *Sabrina,* not with a new spare tire around my waist. But then I observed Famille Chic. The entire family (Monsieur, Madame, and their son) were in great shape; none was overweight. They were living testaments to the famous French paradox. Hmm. If they didn't gain any weight, perhaps I wouldn't either.

And I didn't. Living in France really changed my entire attitude toward food and how to dine well. Not only did I not gain weight while living in Paris but I have maintained my desired weight back home in America even after having had a baby.

To "deprive yourself not" means many things. Deprive yourself not of rich and decadent foods, deprive yourself not of dessert and sweet treats, and deprive yourself not of the experience of fine dining—dining where you totally enjoy yourself and nourish not only your body but your soul as well.

The following are my thoughts and observations on how to dine well, maintain a healthy physique, and deprive yourself not of the joyous experience that is eating.

Attitude and Passion

Attitude is extremely important if you are to enjoy your food and nourish your body. Famille Chic had a very healthy and positive attitude toward food. In the morning Madame Chic would eagerly ask me which of her homemade jams I would prefer, *"Fraise? Ou marmelade d'orange?"*

In the evening when we would all sit together *à table,* we would often discuss the merits of the food we were eating. *Did you know this wine came from this region? The key to this sauce is heavy cream!* Or, *the apricots on this tart are very succulent; yes, we must have this tart again soon.* When the cheese course came out every evening on its humble platter, Monsieur Chic would (without fail) turn to me and offer up a slice of Camembert, proclaiming it to be the *"roi du fromage,"* the king of all cheese.

In America most people groan when a decadent meal is placed before them. "This must have a lot of cream in it! I'll have to hit the gym tomorrow!" or "How many calories do you think *this* has?" During the many dinners I had in France with different people (not just Famille Chic), I never heard any references to calorie counting or thighs expanding. I just heard honest and passionate discussion of the culinary matter at hand.

While having a positive attitude toward food won't stop you from gaining weight, it is the foundation of a healthy relationship with your food and the basis for dining well. If you obsess about what food will do to your figure, your self-deprivation may cause you to overindulge in a particularly decadent meal. Or you might think that because you are going to work it off in the gym the next day, you can have seconds or a bigger portion. If you just have a healthy attitude and small, satisfying portions, you won't have to worry so much.

When Monsieur Chic described Camembert as the *roi du fromage,* he did so with ardor and relish. I found his nightly personification of the cheese to be amusing and sincere. When was the last time you heard someone speak about food passionately and unself-consciously? Monsieur Chic would never say, "This Camembert is the king of all cheeses!" and then, "Unfortunately it's going to go straight to my love handles." There is absolutely no point in canceling your passion with negativity. You might as well have not said (or eaten) anything at all.

And finally, I will add that proclaiming one's food neurosis to the dinner table is so not chic.

Mindfulness

> *To do two things at once is to do neither.*
> —*Publilius Syrus*

This is one of my favorite quotes on multitasking and it absolutely pertains to eating. Before I lived in Paris, it was not uncommon to see me eating a meal standing up, perhaps at my kitchen counter, with my cell phone lodged between my ear and my shoulder. Or worse yet, in front of the TV. By the time the meal was over, I wouldn't have known I had eaten anything at all.

Famille Chic was very mindful when it came to eating. There was never a moment when I saw a member of their household having a meal where they were not seated, with good posture, napkin on lap, knife and fork in hand, engaging in civilized conversation. And this included breakfast!

The Delicacy Technique

A delicacy can be something rather strange like frogs legs (and yes, I like those), or it can be something rather exciting like black truffles (which I also like). A delicacy is something rare—a treat, if you will.

When I feel as though I'm forgetting to pay attention to what I eat, I employ what I call the delicacy technique.

Think about how you would eat a delicacy if it was placed in front of you. You wouldn't mindlessly jam it into your mouth while you simultaneously check your iPhone, would you? No, you might ooh and ahh a bit, share an excited smile with your dining companion, place a cloth napkin on your lap, carefully pick up your knife and fork, and go in for a taste. You would bring the food to your mouth slowly, taste and savor it. You would discuss it. You would enjoy.

Just imagine if you did this with everything you ate. If you treated mealtime as sacred—no matter what the circumstances.

You would be more likely to eat high-quality foods and fully appreciate them. Your attitude toward food would instantly be healthier. Ultimately you would eat less because you would be attuned to your body and know when you've had enough.

Moderation

My husband and I recently vacationed in Barbados to celebrate the New Year. We stayed in a tiny but luxurious hotel on the waterfront with only a handful of couples and families. There was one French couple at the hotel whom I particularly enjoyed observing. I would have known they were French without their uttering even one word of French. The woman was always presentable yet not overdone. She had a rather insouciant attitude and spent the majority of her time discussing films, politics, and art with her male companion. (Yes, I eavesdropped.) But I was most impressed by her attitude toward food.

Our hotel offered a sumptuous complimentary breakfast buffet every morning. It seemed every possible breakfast choice was available: pancakes, bacon, scrambled eggs, baked beans, hash browns, bagels and cream cheese. I am terrible when it comes to buffets. I want to try it all so that I know what's good, you see. But the Frenchwoman I observed had a large bowl of fruit, plain yogurt, and a cup of coffee every morning . . . completely ignoring the other tempting options! I kept thinking that the fruit was her appetizer and waited for her to get up and grab some pancakes or at least scrambled eggs. But no, that never happened. She was completely unfazed by all the tempting options, enjoying her bowl of fruit and talking passionately with her male companion.

It was her healthy attitude toward food that enabled her to ignore all the tempting options day to day at the breakfast buffet—of that I'm convinced.

Despite the Frenchwoman's example, I would eat a *huge* breakfast every morning. I thought, *Ooh, look at all these goodies! I'd better try them all since I don't get this back at home!* There is something about being on vacation that unleashes the glutton in me, but the French lady I observed did not have the same issue. I'm assuming what she had at the buffet was what she had every day back in France. She seemed to see no reason to change her morning routine. She seemed to be enjoying her breakfast, not depriving herself of the cornucopia of foods offered. Her exercise in moderation gave me a lot to think about.

Presentation

The presentation of food is a vital key to enjoying what you are eating and not overindulging. If your food is presented beautifully, you are more likely to pause and appreciate it, rather than gulp it down. I never paid much attention to how my food was presented before I lived in Paris. But one night, that all changed.

Early one evening, Madame Chic and I were in the kitchen.

The window was open and the warm Parisian breeze accompanied us as we cooked. The dessert we were making was a strawberry tart. I cut and hulled the berries while Madame Chic made her *pâte sucrée* from scratch. I helped her roll it out onto the tart pan, which had gotten a great deal of use over the years. Then Madame Chic instructed me to place the strawberries in the lined tart pan. I eagerly dumped them on top of the crust, rearranged them slightly, and looked up at Madame for the next step.

I was met not with instructions on what to do next but with a look of horror from Madame Chic.

"Jennifer," she said (in French, of course), "*non!* You must arrange the strawberries artfully, symmetrically, all around the dish. *Avec precision!*"

"Oh," I said, looking down at my tart—with its haphazardly arranged strawberries. I thought it looked rather nice—artistic, if one were being kind.

Showing me how it should be done, she proceeded to arrange the berries around the perimeter of the crust, spiraling them in as she went. I finished it off and in the center we placed the nicest-looking berry. Then we proceeded to drizzle on the glaze. Madame Chic, with palpable satisfaction, declared the tart to be "complete."

Making that strawberry tart with Madame Chic was a powerful moment for me. It taught me that no occasion is too small to live well. That perfect little strawberry tart wasn't made for a party or to impress guests. It was made for her family—her husband, son, and me—on a weeknight.

By practicing the best for you and your family on a daily basis, you train your mind and palate to have a healthy attitude toward food and mealtime, and you send the message that you and your family are special enough to receive all the joy that food brings to the table.

Le Petit Déjeuner

Breakfast (or *le petit déjeuner*) in France is a very important ritual. Growing up in California, I knew that breakfast was certainly important, but it never held much ritualistic value. I would usually scarf down a bowl of Cheerios or a piece of toast and call it a morning. Things, I would discover, were very different in Paris.

Monsieur Chic would get up very early every morning to go to work (long before I would get up). He would rise for breakfast at 5:45 a.m. and be out the door by 6:30. Madame Chic would rise before him and have his breakfast prepared by the time he got up. And as you can imagine, breakfast chez Famille Chic was more than a piece of toast and a cup of coffee.

I discovered this on my first morning in the house. After spending a night getting acquainted with the sensation of hunger, I greatly anticipated breakfast. Still in my pajamas (Should I have breakfast before or after I showered and dressed?), I walked timidly back to the kitchen. There I heard the soft hum of the radio and the gentle clanking of dishes. Madame Chic, although in her dressing gown when she first got up to make breakfast for her husband, was now completely dressed and ready for the day (which answered my question about whether I should get dressed before eating breakfast.) She made a comment about how I must like to *faire la grasse matinée* (sleep in). I remember looking at the clock and, seeing it was 7:30 a.m., thinking, *She doesn't know from sleeping in!*

Madame Chic ushered me to the tiny kitchen table, which was adorned with a plethora of delicacies. She asked if I preferred tea or coffee (tea in the morning) and she proceeded to pour my steaming cup of tea into a breakfast bowl. *Oui,* you read that correctly—a bowl.

Yes, I thought perhaps I had gone mad or that the jet lag was getting to me or maybe Madame Chic had run out of teacups, but the following day I noticed it again. Tea was drunk chez Famille Chic out of breakfast bowls. And it wasn't just Famille Chic. I learned that most French people drink their morning beverage out of bowls.

Along with tea, served ceremoniously in a bowl, a typical breakfast would include

- fresh fruit
- *fromage blanc* (a delightful fresh cheese with a consistency similar to yogurt that can be eaten with a sprinkling of sugar)

- a slice from last night's tart (usually apple, apricot, or strawberry—homemade by Madame Chic)
- toasted baguette with jam, otherwise known as a *tartine* (the jam always homemade—strawberry, blackberry, and orange marmalade being her favorites)

Every morning Madame Chic displayed these breakfast options beautifully on the table. Even though we were having breakfast in the less formal kitchen, we would sit with our cloth napkins and good table manners and nourish ourselves for the start of the day. The soothing sounds tinkling from the radio, combined with the comforting aroma of toasted bread, sweet jam, and tea, provided a delightful daily ritual I greatly looked forward to, and it started me off on the right foot for whatever adventures were to come.

Le Recap

- Develop a positive attitude toward food and eating.

- Cultivate your passion for fine food and have fun discussing it!

- Be mindful and present when eating all meals.

- Employ the delicacy technique to create a special dining experience no matter what the circumstance.

- Whether you are having a tuna sandwich or a Gruyère soufflé, make sure the presentation of your food is enticing.

- Employ moderation and restraint while on holiday or at the buffet. (In the long run, you will be glad you did.)

- Strive to eat only quality food.

- Above all . . . enjoy your meals! We spend so much of our lives eating. Revel in it—have fun and take pleasure in the dining experience.

Chapter 3

EXERCISE IS A PART OF LIFE, NOT A CHORE

The first time I visited Madame Bohemienne I was in for a surprise. Madame Bohemienne was the host mother of my boyfriend from California who was also in my study abroad program. He had told me about how wonderful she was and that he was getting on really well with her two sons. They all wanted to meet me, and so I was invited to dinner.

I took the metro all the way from the Sixteenth Arrondissement to the Eleventh Arrondissement (which takes nearly an hour), walked up several hilly, cobblestoned streets, and finally reached their apartment building. By the time I got there, I was already out of breath. But my journey had really just begun. The apartment of Famille Bohemienne was several floors up . . . and there was no elevator.

I did the only thing I could do. I braced myself and made the climb. I arrived in a state of complete disarray. Not only was I out of breath but I was rather sweaty. (It was cold outside, so I was wearing a heavy winter coat.) I was dumbfounded by the fact that Famille Bohemienne could get by with living so high up without an elevator.

How did they bring up bags of groceries? What happened when they moved in? How on earth would they move out? Did she and her sons climb this mountain of stairs every day—several times a day—to get to their home?

Yes, they did—and they didn't think twice about it. In fact, they were rather amused at my astonishment that they didn't have an elevator.

Living in Paris awakened me to the rather obvious fact that I was lazy. Before living in France I would *never* take more than a couple of flights of stairs if an elevator was an option (which it almost always is in America).

Life in Paris is an active one—exercise is a part of everyday life. Famille Bohemienne would walk up those flights of stairs every day without a struggle. They were extremely fit. In addition to climbing the stairs, Madame Bohemienne walked all over the city—running errands, going to work, and visiting friends. I believe the family had one car—but rarely used it.

Famille Chic also had only one car. The only time they used it was to visit their vacation home in Brittany or when their son occasionally went on a night out.

Daily Shopping as Exercise

For shopping, Madame Chic would bring along a cart and fill it with items from each shop she visited. She only purchased what she would need for that day. She preferred to visit specialty shops like the local *pâtisserie, charcuterie,* or *boulangerie* instead of going to one giant *supermarché,* because the quality of goods she got at the specialty shops was superior to what one would find in a supermarket, and she got more exercise by going to more than one shop.

One day when I had the morning off from school, I accompanied Madame Chic on her daily shopping trip. It was a very cold morning with a shockingly brisk breeze. (Remember I am from Southern California, so my seemingly amplified depiction of the cold weather comes from a place of truth!) Madame Chic and I were bundled up and walking down a wide street in the Sixteenth where the specialty shops were found. She toted along her compact shopping cart covered in red canvas and with expert adroitness zigzagged into each shop with me following one step behind. There was never a coherent system of payment in these shops. In other words, there was no line. The local French people did not queue up to order and pay. They just haphazardly made their way to the vendors, chimed out an animated *"Bonjour!"* and ordered what they needed. (I will never understand the complete disregard in France for the concept of lining up. Not queuing up stresses me out! Where is the sense of order? It feels like total anarchy! But that is another story . . .)

I can't even remember what we purchased that day, I was so cold and exhausted. Baguettes, veal chops, fresh fruit—it didn't matter. I couldn't believe Madame Chic did this almost every day. Back in California I would hop in my car once a week, do one giant shop at the grocery store, and feel slightly put out that I even had to haul the bags from the car to my front door. In California any sign of bad weather is an excuse to hurl all plans out the window and stay home by the fireplace instead!

When I mentioned these observations to Madame Chic, she laughed. "It's good to get fresh air, Jennifer—one mustn't be lazy!" I remember her saying.

One Mustn't Be Lazy

Yes, one mustn't be lazy. I never thought of myself as being lazy before living in Paris. But the more I thought about it, the more I realized how inactive my life had been. In Paris I would take the metro to class every day—which took nearly an hour, as the Sixteenth Arrondissement is on the edge of the city—and then walk to my classes. After class my friends and I would usually break loose and explore the city. We visited museums, trekked to interesting cafés, walked by the Seine. We did all of the typical (and rather wonderful) things that people do when visiting Paris. Sometimes we would walk so far, we'd end up on the other side of the city.

Back home in California I rarely walked anywhere. Los Angeles is not a walking city in general, as everything is so spread out and there is no major public transit option like the Paris Métro. But I am not making excuses. There were several places I could have walked to but chose to drive to instead. I thought exercise was for the gym only. Why would I waste precious time walking or running somewhere when I could drive and atone for my laziness the next day in kickboxing class?

And speaking of kickboxing class—neither Famille Chic nor Famille Bohemienne went to the gym to work out. They had a different attitude toward fitness. They got their exercise by cleaning their houses, walking instead of driving, taking the stairs, and running errands on foot. That is not to say that the gym is bad. If you happen to be the sort of person who loves going to the gym (and I do know this rare breed of human), then by all means, carry on! But if you find yourself constantly experiencing guilt trips because you have not made it to the gym, perhaps the gym is not for you.

Positive Body Image

If Madame Chic or Madame Bohemienne had a negative body image, I wouldn't have known, as they didn't complain about their bodies or about being "fat" like so many men and women do in America. Just as the French have a positive attitude toward eating, they have a positive attitude toward the body and fitness.

Famille Chic, Famille Bohemienne, and their friends simply resolved to maintain an active life so that they could enjoy things like culinary decadence on a daily basis, without guilt.

That said, these women did not hold themselves to the same standards that my friends do in Los Angeles. Madame Chic was not rake thin. She had five children and had a full, beautiful figure. She was not overweight—she just had curves and she embraced them. Madame Bohemienne was quite thin (she had two children), but that was her inherent physique. Each of these women embraced her body type. Madame Chic would never be waiflike. To fight her curves would be absurd. Conversely, Madame Bohemienne would never have major curves. She embraced her thin, boyish figure. They were content with what they were given and worked with it.

Techniques

Now, we can't all live in Paris and be French, so here are some creative ways to incorporate exercise into your everyday life no matter where you live.

Create an active challenge for yourself every day.

This challenge should be custom-tailored to your particular needs and to your life. A few years after living in Paris, I moved into an apartment in Santa Monica with my friend Anjali. Her apartment was on the third floor of the building. There were elevators in the building but I opted—like Madame Bohemienne—to walk up the stairs. I did this almost every time—even if I had groceries or something else to carry. I created an active challenge for myself. I probably climbed those stairs at least four times a day. Multiply that by 365 days a year and you see where I'm going . . . Walking up those stairs was great for my legs, my derrière, and my morale. When I was carrying things, it was great for my arms!

In the French film *Si c'était lui . . .*, actress Carole Bouquet portrays a modern and successful Frenchwoman who seems to have it all. She lives in a beautiful apartment in Paris with her young son and has a very successful career and a dedicated boyfriend. Every day when she walks up the stairs to her apartment, she doesn't just walk, she walks briskly, always repeating the last few steps by walking up backward, presumably to keep her taut derrière looking, well, taut.

I now live with my husband, children, and dog in a multi-level town home. Since I no longer have to climb three flights of stairs to get to my front door, I decided to customize a routine tailored to my new living circumstances. When I am feeling as though I haven't gotten enough exercise, I walk up and down all four levels of stairs in our town home ten times. I really get into it and my Chihuahua, Gatsby, likes to follow me as I go, making a very entertaining spectacle for those who are watching. I create a challenge for myself and complete it. The best part about this form of exercise? It's free and usually quite inspiring!

Explore your neighborhood.

Having a sense of adventure and being open to exploring your neighborhood is critical. Certainly if one lives in Paris or any other major metropolitan city, it is exciting to explore your own neighborhood, but what about for the rest of us? When I arrived in California after living in Paris, I felt let down. Paris was such a beautiful city—there was so much to explore—how could my new neighborhood in Los Angeles compete? I'd given up on my own city before really trying.

Then after I had my baby, I decided to walk when running errands, like Madame Chic in Paris. I started to explore my neighborhood in Santa Monica and have been extremely pleased with the results. I have become acquainted with so many tiny shops I might not have known existed had I not taken to walking in my own city. I discovered that I live near a major grocery store and also near many tiny ethnic shops, with lovely selections of produce and meats, as well as bakeries! I never would have discovered these local delights if I had not ventured out on foot. I am able to frequent these shops about every other day to do the shopping. As a result, the food I cook is fresher and I also get more exercise. I've also befriended many of my neighbors and gained a stronger sense of community.

Make your leisure time more active.

In Paris my leisure time was more active, less sedentary. Famille Chic did not have a sofa and did not snack, so in my downtime I certainly wasn't lying down, watching TV, and eating potato chips. I was walking by the Seine, going to museums and cafés. I was out on adventures . . . I was exploring. I was also exercising and keeping fit—although I didn't realize it at the time. By making your leisure time more active, you set a standard for yourself and soon can become addicted to being active. Your days begin to feel incomplete if you don't schedule a walk, or if you don't venture to your local café to read or socialize.

Have a domestic workout.

Even though they had the means, Madame Chic and Madame Bohemienne did not employ cleaners. They did all the housework themselves. I'm not necessarily advocating this (I say if you can afford a cleaner, then employ one!), but it has to be said that doing a lot of the housework yourself can keep your body fit. Housework is an excellent way to incorporate exercise into your life. Most of us have to do housework in some form or another. Why not get the most you can out of it?

I normally don't advocate multitasking, but cleaning and exercising at the same time is an exception. Cleaning the house burns calories, but adding a few creative moves can help keep your body svelte. Do lunges while you vacuum, squats when you dust chair legs, and inject a miniature fitness regime in your cleaning routine.

For example, try speed-cleaning your home every day to keep it looking presentable. Set a time limit for yourself. Try ten minutes. Play motivational music and really go for it. Get your heart rate up. Scrub, push, mop, wipe, straighten—or whatever it is that needs to be done. You will burn calories and beautify your space at the same time.

Or if you have a major task that needs to be done, such as polishing the floor, make it work to your advantage. I am reminded of my favorite film, *Amélie,* in which Amélie's mother polishes the floor with her slippered feet. She does this with relish and goes at the task with verve and pleasure, while simultaneously toning her legs and derrière.

Cleaning *and* exercising are not two words that normally bring one joy. So if you plan on combining them, try to make the experience as pleasurable as possible so you will be encouraged to continue. Don your favorite gloves or apron (I'm not just talking to the ladies—men, you can do this too! Hercule Poirot, James Bond, and my own father—all stylish men in their own right—have donned aprons to get work done), play motivational music, or promise yourself a treat after you finish. Do whatever you can to make the experience pleasurable.

And when you're not doing housework . . .

- Dance! I love to put on music in the morning and dance with my children. They find it quite amusing, I get a good workout in, and we all laugh. It's a mood booster.
- Park your car as far away as possible from your destination to encourage more walking.
- Take the dog for a walk. Choose a new route every day so you don't get bored.
- Always take the stairs in lieu of the elevator.
- Do leg lifts while watching TV.
- Explore alternative forms of exercise such as yoga, tai chi, or chi gong.

In short, don't be stagnant. If you are open and creative, you can incorporate exercise into almost every aspect of your daily routine as a complement to, or in lieu of, working out in a gym.

Le Recap

- Incorporate exercise into your daily tasks (like grocery shopping and doing household chores).

- Develop a positive body image. Focus on the good things about your body.

- Create an active challenge for yourself every day.

- Explore your neighborhood on foot or on bicycle.

- Make your leisure time more active.

- And most important, never be lazy! Laziness is not chic.

Part 2
STYLE AND
BEAUTY

Chapter 4

LIBERATE YOURSELF WITH THE TEN-ITEM WARDROBE

When Famille Chic first welcomed me into their home, I sat with Madame and Monsieur Chic and a cup of tea as we all introduced ourselves. They asked me questions about my studies and my life in America and said that they wanted me to be comfortable in their home. A sort of *"Mi casa es su casa"* conversation—but in French! After I finished my cup of tea, Madame Chic kindly mentioned that I might want some time to myself to rest before dinner and offered to show me my bedroom. This was the moment I had been anticipating. Their apartment, thus far, was beautiful and I was sure my bedroom would be no exception.

It was lovely. There was a single bed with a green velvet coverlet, stately floor-to-ceiling windows hung with botanical draperies and providing a view of a picturesque courtyard, a desk perfectly adequate for my studies, and a very tiny freestanding wardrobe in which to store my clothes.

Attendez.

A tiny freestanding wardrobe?

It had all been going so well until that moment. I remember panicking slightly as I regarded my two large, overstuffed suitcases. Where was the closet? I opened the wardrobe doors—there was only a handful of hangers inside. Now I really panicked. Was this where I was supposed to keep all of my clothes for the next six months?

I was in denial at the time, but the answer to that question was undeniably *oui!*

I quickly learned that such a tiny space was perfectly adequate for the storage needs of Famille Chic. They each had a wardrobe of about ten items. Monsieur Chic, Madame Chic, and their son had really nice clothes; they just happened to wear the same things in rotation—over and over again.

For example, Madame Chic's wardrobe for winter consisted

of three or four wool skirts, four cashmere sweaters, and three silk blouses. (Madame Chic rarely wore trousers.) She had a uniform of sorts and wore it well.

Monsieur Chic's wardrobe consisted of two gray suits, one navy suit, two or three sweaters, about four collared shirts, and a couple of ties. The same went for their son, although he rarely wore suits—mainly collared shirts and sweaters. Their son was the only one in the family to occasionally wear jeans.

And Famille Chic weren't the only Parisians who needed nothing more than a capsule wardrobe. I remember discussing, with dismay, the subject with my fellow students from America. Not one of us had a large closet space in our rooms. Which led me to wonder—do the French rely on a ten-item wardrobe for lack of closet space? Or is the lack of closet space a result of their needing only a ten-item wardrobe? Either way, it didn't matter. I had to find a way to house my ridiculously large American wardrobe for the next six months.

While in Paris, I observed the beauty of the ten-item wardrobe. I noticed that the French people whom I saw on a regular basis (mainly my professors, shopkeepers, and friends such as Famille Bohemienne and, of course, Famille Chic) wore the same clothes in heavy rotation—unapologetically and with great panache.

In America, one would be embarrassed to wear the same thing twice in one week, let alone three times. But in France, it is no big deal. In fact, everyone does it!

I started to notice it in French films as well. While the female characters in American films make a ridiculous number of *Sex and the City*–esque wardrobe changes, in French films, more often than not, you will see the female lead wear the same outfit *at least* twice during the course of the film. You would *never* encounter this in American films unless the filmmaker wants to make a point that the character is poor or depressed.

I recently saw the French film *Je ne dis pas non,* where Sylvie Testud's character wears the same thing for practically the entire movie—or the same three things—even though the film takes place over several months.

This all got me thinking. There was such a drastic difference between the closets in France and the closets in America. I have seen my fair share of closets in America—closets of my friends, closets of my family, and closets on those reality TV shows about people who hoard—and I have noticed one very blaring trait: *American closets are stuffed to the brim.* We have so many clothes! Is this a good thing? Are we happy? Do we absolutely love everything in our closets? What is the quality of the clothes we are buying? And most important, why were we standing in front of our jam-packed closets every morning complaining that we have nothing to wear?

Back in America I decided to try out my very own ten-item wardrobe. What started out as an experiment (and a reluctant one, at that) became a major turning point for me. Many people can be intimidated by the idea of the ten-item wardrobe, and frankly, I don't blame them. It can be a drastic thing going from a large wardrobe to only around ten core items, but believe me, this exercise is powerful—even if you only do it for a week. You can learn a lot about yourself and your style—what your wardrobe needs, why you resist wearing your nicest things (I still have a fighting urge to "save" my best clothes for later), and how you want to present yourself as a person.

The Definition of a Ten-Item Wardrobe

Don't panic. You don't need to take the ten-item wardrobe literally. Remember, Famille Chic were not the sort to beat themselves up over a regime—certainly not over diet or exercise and definitely not over their wardrobe. So do what works for you. The point of the ten-item wardrobe is to free yourself from a jam-packed closet full of ill-fitting, underused, or poor-quality clothing. Your ultimate goal is to create a wardrobe that you love, in which every item of clothing speaks to who you are, and to create a space for your clothes to breathe—by eliminating clutter.

Your wardrobe should consist of ten core items, give or take a few, but those ten items do not include outerwear (coats, jackets, blazers), occasionwear (cocktail dresses, evening gowns, special day dresses, etc.), accessories (scarves, gloves, hats, wraps), shoes, and what I call under shirts—mainly tee shirts, tank tops, or chemises that you wear as layers or underneath a sweater or blazer. (I found it necessary to have several of these to avoid having to do laundry every other day and to prolong the wear on things like cashmere sweaters).

Also the ten-item wardrobe is assessed each season and items are exchanged accordingly. For example, if you do this experiment in the summer, you will not have three cashmere sweaters in your ten items. Those can go in storage and you can usher in three summer dresses to replace the sweaters, or whatever suits your lifestyle.

Clear Out the Wardrobe Clutter

In order to pick your ten items, you must first clear the clutter from your closet. It is very important to physically clean out your wardrobe so that when you are finished, you have only your ten items (plus extras previously discussed) hanging in your closet. It is very easy to think you'll wear your ten items during the experiment but still keep your other clothes jammed in the closet "just in case" or because you are too lazy and can't find anywhere else to put your clothes. But the act of getting rid of all your excess clothing or storing it elsewhere is very powerful and prevents you from cheating.

During the process of clearing my closet clutter, I took the plunge and got rid of 70 percent of my wardrobe. This, for me, was a tremendous accomplishment. It was easy, though, because I took the time to assess each item. I threw everything on my bed, and one by one I examined each garment, asking myself a few key questions that helped me to let go.

Wardrobe Assessment Questions

Do I still like this? In many instances I was holding on to something because I had paid a lot of money for it—not because I actually liked it.

Do I ever wear this? I had many clothes that I simply did not wear. Some I hadn't worn in over two years! I knew I never would wear them again, but for some reason I couldn't let go.

Does it still fit and flatter me? People gain or lose weight, have babies, and get older—bodies change! It is important not to be in denial about your current body shape. Dress yourself for your current body—not the body you used to have or wish you had.

Does this article of clothing still reflect who I am? This is a very powerful question, and in most instances my answer was a resounding *no*. I was holding on to blouses and skirts that I had purchased in my early twenties. (I even found a few baby doll dresses—yikes!) A lot has changed since then. I am a wife and mother. My tastes are more refined and sophisticated. Those clothes were not right for the *new* me.

I realize you might not be ready to purge everything the first time around. That is okay. After you weed out the items you know you no longer want, I suggest storing clothes that are not in the chosen ten in space-saving bags or a container in another room or in your garage. Just keep them out of your sight. You might find you go an entire year without thinking about them at all, in which case you know you could probably do without them.

Customizing Your Ten-Item Wardrobe

Now that you've cleared out the clutter, it's time to customize your ten-item wardrobe. This will all depend on who you are, where you live, and what sort of lifestyle you lead. An attorney in Manhattan will, of course, have a drastically different ten-item wardrobe than a stay-at-home mom in Atlanta.

Think about what your day usually consists of. Board meetings? PTA meetings? Working from home? Riding your bike? Also take into consideration the season (snow, perpetual rain, warm sunshine?) and of course your style and personality (fashion forward, classic minimalism, bohemian?).

My ten-item wardrobe has been tailored to fit my particular life situation: I am a mother with two small children, but I still like to look pulled together, so the majority of my wardrobe is casual sportswear with a slight dressed-up edge. I live in Southern California, which has a temperate climate even in the winter.

I mainly spend my days taking care of the home and children, going to playdates, writing, and going on walks. My choices for the ten-item wardrobe reflect my lifestyle.

Here are some examples of ten-item wardrobes. Every item in this selection of clothing can be mixed and matched, thus creating many sartorial possibilities—a must for any capsule wardrobe.

Sample Ten-Item Wardrobe for Spring/Summer

sea-green silk top

tan sheer blouse

navy and white striped sailor tee

beige crewneck sweater

sea-foam button-down tie cardigan

lightweight pleated black trousers

tailored black high-waisted shorts

sea-green A-line skirt

tan khaki pencil skirt

white and/or dark blue jeans

Sample Ten-Item Wardrobe for Fall/Winter

3 cashmere sweaters in beige, cream, and black

3 silk blouses

1 button-down white shirt

tailored dark wool trousers

black wool skirt

black skinny or boot-cut jeans

My One-Month Experiment

The following are some observations I jotted down when I adhered strictly to the ten-item wardrobe experiment for one whole month.

Opening my closet in the morning makes me happy. Not only is it wonderful to see my clothes hanging so neatly in their own space (not jam-packed next to each other), but it makes me inordinately happy not to wonder what to wear for the day. There are so few options, it only takes me a minute to make a choice. Also, having a clutter-free closet boosts my mood. (It must be the feng shui of it all).

My desire to shop has not been strong. I did not expect this reaction in the slightest. I thought that after the first week with my ten-item wardrobe I would be begging for someone to take me to Nordstrom. Not so. There is something marvelous about having so little hanging in my closet; I am not in a rush to drop a lot of money and fill it up with clutter anytime soon. I know the urge to shop will return, but when it does, I am hoping that I will peruse potential purchases with a very discerning eye.

When I do go shopping, I note that it is now liberating. I normally never come home from a shopping trip without having purchased something. Now, I am interested in more expensive, quality pieces. I am more comfortable with window-shopping for research purposes and not buying. I know that the next purchase I make will be something of quality and that I need to take my time before making that investment.

Acknowledging when an article of clothing is past its prime becomes easier. Recently I spotted a woman, who was wearing leggings, bend over and hug an acquaintance. She was in a room full of people, and when she bent over, she revealed three rather large holes in her leggings that exposed her backside! Clearly this is a woman who could have benefited from analyzing her wardrobe. If she had, she might have realized that her leggings were past their prime and she could have avoided such embarrassment. This poor woman's wardrobe malfunction scared me into analyzing my own wardrobe. I noticed that one of my favorite "extra" shirts, a gray tee from Splendid, was starting to look a bit sad. After one too many washings, it hung on my body in a very unflattering shape and just looked a little the worse for wear. I believe the pre-ten-item-wardrobe me would have ignored the fact and stored it away just because it was kind of expensive (for a tee shirt), but the post-ten-item-wardrobe me recognized that for my little gray tee, retirement was imminent—and I got rid of it!

The ability to mix and match your clothing and create many possibilities is of the utmost importance. You should be able to pair every item with every other item in your ten-item wardrobe. This is the only way to avoid becoming bored, eventually growing to loathe your clothing, and uttering those familiar words "I have nothing to wear!"

If you choose your ten-item wardrobe carefully, you can force yourself to use only the best things you have. Over time you will become accustomed to doing so and stop saving your best for "later."

To preserve your nice clothing while doing housework or other chores, wear an apron around the house. This was Madame Chic's secret to keeping her clothes looking fresh while simultaneously doing a lot of housework and cooking.

Getting behind in doing the laundry or dropping off the dry cleaning is not an option. This can be a problem if you're having a hectic week. I had a week where I got very behind with household chores (laundry included) and was running on empty with regard to my wardrobe. I had to pull some items from my reserves to get by. Also, dropping off dry cleaning must be coordinated so that all your dry cleaning is not out at the same time. If you do not have the laundry/dry cleaning routine under control, adding more than ten core items (twenty or twenty-five, for example) is probably the best solution.

If your fashion budget is on the lower end, avoid overspending on the core items. You do not need to make all of your ten items investment pieces. Save the big splurges for coats, shoes, sunglasses, handbags, cocktail dresses, jeans, watches, and jewelry. These items will last you a long time, so quality is of the utmost importance. Also, if the above-mentioned items are quality, they can really dress up a moderately priced outfit and make it look quite expensive.

If you are still resisting the ten-item wardrobe but are curious about its benefits, try it out the next time you go on vacation. Let the length of your trip determine what you pack. For example, if you are going away for a long weekend, bring only two or three outfits. If you are going away for two weeks, try packing a ten-item wardrobe. You will experience the same benefits you would if you were conducting the challenge in your own home and will have much less luggage to tote around (which is always a good thing).

Going forward, you should adapt your wardrobe so that it is right for you. If you are doing the experiment to the letter and are using only your ten core items and are having a wardrobe revelation, carry on! If you find that you need to add more pieces into your capsule wardrobe to make it really work for you, then that is okay too. The exercise is extreme, and even though Madame Chic and her family truly employed the ten-item wardrobe, it might not be right for you. I hope you will take the best that this challenge has to offer and become more discerning toward the clothing you bring into your wardrobe. You will look at your wardrobe the way you look at your home and not allow clutter into it. And ultimately, you will get one step closer to defining your true style.

Le Recap

- Clear out the clutter in your wardrobe. Be brutal!

- Store away any seasonal clothes that are not appropriate for the current season.

- Commit to doing the ten-item wardrobe experiment for a set period of time. (One month worked for me.)

- Choose your ten items. (Remember these do not include outerwear, occasionwear, accessories, shoes, and layering shirts.)

- After doing the strict experiment, note what works and does not work for you and add or subtract items as needed.

- Most important, enjoy the process. The whole point of the exercise is to help you love every item in your wardrobe and always have something appropriate and presentable to wear.

Chapter 5

FIND YOUR TRUE STYLE

Do you remember the trip I took with Madame Chic to run errands? Well, along with learning how Madame Chic kept fit by visiting her local specialty stores, I discovered something else that day . . .

I was rather pleased with my relationship with Madame Chic. She was still an enigma to me, being rather formidable and somewhat intimidating at times. She wasn't warm and embracing like Madame Bohemienne, but she did seem to like me. I suppose I just wasn't used to her formal nature. I did enjoy the time I spent with her, and she was patient with my use of the French language. On that day when she asked me if I would like to accompany her on her daily shopping trip, I felt honored: she seemed to be taking me under her wing!

So I was shocked when only one block away from the house she turned to me and said rather bluntly, "That sweater does not look good on you."

"Pardon?" I remember asking. I looked down at my spring-green sweater set from Banana Republic that was partially obscured by my heavy winter coat. Surely I couldn't have heard her right.

She repeated her statement.

"Really?" I asked, this time in English. I felt wounded. "But it's silk and cashmere blend!"

"No, it's not the quality that disturbs me, Jennifer," Madame Chic said, eyeing the offending sweater set with intensity. "It's the color. It does not suit you at all. It washes you out. You look . . . *sallow.*"

Ouch. I remember thinking, *I look sallow?* I was shocked that Madame Chic had been so blunt. My friends and I told each other we looked good *no matter what*. And if someone looked bad? We wouldn't say anything at all. (After all, if you don't have anything nice to say . . .) *Mon Dieu,* I must have looked *terrible* if Madame Chic actually had the guts to tell me so!

She could see the crestfallen look on my face. "Don't be upset, Jennifer!" she said. "It's just an observation. As a woman you must know what colors look the best on you. How are you to know if no one tells you?"

This was true. I again looked down at the sweater set. It had actually been a gift from a friend. I didn't particularly like the color myself. I wouldn't have chosen it. Come to think of it, I would never have chosen a sweater set in the first place. Sweater sets just weren't me. But this was free . . . It was a gift! And it was a cashmere/silk blend from Banana Republic!

I asked her tentatively, "What colors do you think *would* look good on me? Not green, obviously."

"Mais pas du tout!" Madame Chic exclaimed. "You would look ravishing in emerald green, mint green, and sea-foam green—just not that particular shade." She eyed the unfortunate sweater set again as she said this. I decided to button my coat so as to avoid any more pitying looks.

In addition, Madame Chic asserted that I would look good in aubergine, royal blue, ruby red, black, cream, plum, lavender, melon, and salmon pink. In fact, she told me I would look great in most colors except for certain yellows and that spring green!

My icy wall of defense began to thaw as Madame Chic imparted one more bit of wisdom before we tackled the chaos that was the Parisian markets. She said, "You must pay very close attention to what enhances your beauty and what detracts from it. It is a must for every woman."

Believe it or not, I had never thought about enhancing my beauty with clothing before that moment. I looked how I looked. I didn't have a negative self-image by any means, but I never actually thought about making calculated style choices to make myself more beautiful. Of course this is in the back of any person's mind when shopping for clothes—we all want to look good. But *how much* thought do we put into what we wear? Do we wear clothes simply because we must to avoid being cold (or being arrested for indecent exposure)? Or do we dress as an art—as part of an act of seduction—not just for the opposite sex but for ourselves, to entice ourselves with our beauty. And what detracts from our beauty? Do we know what these things are? Or do we need a Madame Chic to tell us?

Why We Wear the Things We Do

So later that night I ruminated. Why was I wearing that sweater set in the first place? Sweater sets were not things I particularly liked . . . Neither was the color pea-soup green—which my sweater set was (yes, in my mind it went from spring green to pea-soup green). I suppose I wore it because it was given to me as a gift, but surely that couldn't have been the *only* reason? Perhaps I needed to become more selective about what I put on my body.

The first two chapters in this book recommend that you take the time to really think about the food you consume. It makes sense to be equally thoughtful about the clothes you wear. In other words, if you are careful to eat only the best foods, then you should be equally choosy about what you adorn your body with. Why wear something that you don't totally love—that doesn't speak of your essence and present your true style?

Too often we get into the trap of keeping clothes and wearing them for the wrong reasons. Maybe something was given to us by a loved one and we would feel too guilty not to wear it. Maybe the item was bought in a moment of bad judgment and we don't want to waste the money spent, so we wear it, even though we don't like it. Maybe we would like to think something looks good on us because it is part of a trend that we fancy or it looks good on a model or celebrity. None of those reasons are the right reasons.

We should only wear clothes because we love them, they look good on us, and they speak to who we are as people. No exceptions.

Define Your Style

My conversation with Madame Chic that day made me realize I needed to cultivate my sense of style. Until then, my chaotic closet had housed a rather schizophrenic wardrobe, a mix of bohemian, preppy, urban, and who knows what other looks.

Frenchwomen really seem to know their style and weave it into their lives masterfully. Madame Chic had a signature look. Her style was classic and conservative. She liked cashmere sweaters, A-line skirts, and flats or low heels. She was completely comfortable and at ease in her look. It was effortless.

Madame Bohemienne's style was entirely hers as well. She loved (can you guess?) bohemian-style, flowy skirts and three-quarter-sleeve or sleeveless tops. She rarely strayed from her look. Both of these women knew who they were and were completely comfortable with it. I can't imagine either one of them standing in front of her wardrobe frazzled because she couldn't decide what to wear.

Whether consciously or subconsciously, Madame Chic and Madame Bohemienne had defined their true styles. Madame Chic was not the sort to experiment with trends. It was not her style. This, I can imagine, simplified her life, sartorially speaking. She knew what looked good on her, what she felt comfortable in, and (as she so blatantly reminded me on our walk) what brought out her beauty. I got the sense that she loved every article of clothing in her wardrobe.

It's All about Labels (but Not the Kind You Think!)

Loving all the clothes in your wardrobe is achievable if, like Madame Chic, you are able to define your true style. Let's try an exercise. If you could describe your style in one or two words right now, could you do it?

Attaching a label to your style is a powerful way to zero in on who you are, stylistically speaking. Some people might be put off by labeling their look, but a style can be anything from classic to trendy to eclectic. Don't worry. Nothing is set in stone. You can change your label at any time.

If you are a fashion rebel and like an unconventional high-fashion look like Fan Bingbing or Isabella Blow, your label could be *eccentric chic*. If you like a sophisticated and elegant look like Catherine, Duchess of Cambridge, you could label your look *ladylike chic*. Get creative with labeling your look. You don't have to stick to the generic labels we've all heard before (like bohemian or preppy). Your label can be unique!

For example, I would label my current style as *laid-back luxe*. *Laid-back* because I live mainly in California and like to wear casual sportswear with a dressed-up edge. *Luxe* because I enjoy luxurious textures like silks, cashmeres, or ultrasoft cottons and like to pair my (mainly minimalistic) clothing with my best jewelry. Also, my family and I spend a few months each year in Europe (primarily England), so my casual California wardrobe has to work with the more dressed-up protocol of London life. A typical outfit for me would be skinny jeans, ballet flats, a fitted blazer, and a silk top, or a jersey dress with embellished sandals and a voluminous scarf. In these two examples, the jeans and the jersey dress are the laid-back elements, and the blazer, silk top, sandals, and scarf are the luxe elements. Does *laid-back luxe* exist as a technical fashion term? I have no idea! But I use the expression to define my style.

Also, do your research by looking at public figures or people you see on the street. Who influences and inspires your look? Stylewise I am inspired by Sofia Coppola, Audrey Tautou, Marion Cotillard, Michelle Williams, and Catherine, Duchess of Cambridge.

Once you label your style, you can do research and find out which designers cater to your look. For example, if you classify your look as *ladylike chic* and like to wear tailored coats, elegant dresses, and feminine suits, your go-to brands might be Nanette Lepore, Catherine Malandrino, Diane von Furstenberg, and Jenny Packham. For my laid-back luxe look I get a lot of my clothes from A.P.C., BCBG Max Azria, Diane von Furstenberg, Ferragamo, James Perse, J Brand, J. Crew, London Sole, Nanette Lepore, Rebecca Taylor, Velvet, and Vince (amongst others). I know that when I walk into one of those boutiques, I will probably find something that would fit nicely into my wardrobe.

Presenting Yourself to the World

By defining your style, you are deciding how you would like to present yourself to the world. After you label your style, you might discover that your label doesn't actually represent the current you. For example, if your style was preppy when you were in college, but it is now ten years later and you feel bored with your uniform of polo shirts and khakis, it might be time to explore different styles. I believe that every ten years (at least!) we should reevaluate our look. Certainly what a woman wore in her early twenties would not be appropriate in her midforties. As we age, we grow wiser, more sophisticated, and (hopefully) more prosperous. Our clothing should reflect that.

Labeling your style can also help you avoid buying items that don't go with anything else. We've all bought that random thing that doesn't quite go with the rest of our clothes. You know you've done it when you begin thinking you need to purchase other items to go with it in order to make it work. Of course, the reason it doesn't work in the first place is, it's not your style.

Now that I have defined my true style, I save a lot of money and time. I basically ignore the trends and stick with what I know and like. Clothes shopping is a joy. I just see what my favorite brands put out each season and purchase a few key elements to enhance and supplement my wardrobe.

Know Thyself

To answer a question I posed earlier, we do *not* need a Madame Chic to tell us what detracts from our beauty. We all *know* what our style is—what makes us feel good. When I wore that green sweater set, I knew, deep down, that it wasn't for me. It did not make me feel beautiful. But I decided to keep it and wear it, for all the wrong reasons. Life is short. Every day is so important, why waste it wearing something that isn't *you*?

Every day we have instincts that help us make the right

decisions—whom to trust, which route to take, what to have for lunch. We have these instincts about our clothing too. The question is, do you ignore your instinct? And if so, why?

For example, perhaps you live in a cold climate and your wardrobe consists of mainly dark colors like black, navy, and gray because you think they are appropriate for winter weather. You may long to wear vibrant colors but you find yourself giving all kinds of excuses for wearing dark colors: *I don't want to draw unnecessary attention to myself on the street by wearing a red coat in a sea of black.* Or *I need to wear dark colors because they won't show stains as easily if I get splashed by a rain puddle on the way to work.* Or *I've heard that people look more chic when wearing black.*

You might be listening to these excuses more than your gut instinct, which is really saying, *I would feel happier and more beautiful wearing color.* If this example resonates with you, do an experiment and go with your gut instinct. Get in touch with what you really want to say with your look. By knowing yourself and really listening to your inner voice, you can begin to embrace your unique beauty.

Bien dans Sa Peau

The French expression *bien dans sa peau* means to be "comfortable in your skin." So many of the women I observed in France embodied this expression. They were confident and effortless. Madame Chic and Madame Bohemienne were both *bien dans* _leur peau_. Even though they were wildly different, they each performed their roles in life with ease and grace. They did not appear to be neurotic about any aspect of their lives. I'm sure they had their off days just like any other person, but for the most part they embodied happiness and stability. I believe knowing your style and sticking to it contributes to this blissful state of being—of not feeling self-conscious. Of not second-guessing yourself. Of feeling assertive and beautiful.

Le Recap

- Only wear clothes because you love them, they look great on you, and they reflect who you are.

- Define your true style to help guide you when shopping.

- Think of how you want to present yourself to the world every time you get dressed.

- Listen to your instinct about your style. Deep down you know if something works or doesn't work.

Chapter 6

PERFECT
LE NO-MAKEUP LOOK

n Paris I loved to sit for hours at a café with a café crème and people-watch. And while Frenchmen were very fun to observe (for other reasons), I equally enjoyed watching the women—who, for the most part, looked polished yet natural. Were they wearing makeup or weren't they? It was hard to tell, but their cheeks had a natural glow, their eyes were slightly defined, and their lips were usually a pretty, earthy shade. They had, in essence, a no-makeup look.

Madame Chic and Madame Bohemienne both employed *le no-makeup look*—as do most women in France. Madame Chic, for example, always looked polished but not in a contrived way.

I could never actually tell if she was wearing makeup. I knew she wore lipstick. Madame Chic was a lady of a certain age and wore lipstick to brighten her complexion. She generally would wear red on her lips but at times would also wear soft pink. She occasionally wore mascara to highlight and define her eyes. But the fact that I otherwise couldn't decide whether she was wearing makeup was a testament to her adroitness in applying it. Her face always looked clean and healthy. I'm guessing if she wore lipstick and mascara, she also wore foundation and probably blush. Her cheeks always had a healthy glow, but that could have been from her active lifestyle—one can never tell!

Madame Bohemienne employed *le no-makeup look* as well. And as Madame Bohemienne's style was less chic and more, well, bohemian, it is quite possible that she actually didn't wear makeup. Her skin tone was even, her face bright, but again, it wasn't clearly obvious whether she enhanced her beauty with makeup. She loved to wear pink lipstick, but that was the only makeup I could detect.

Mystery is the very essence of *le no-makeup look*—its entire raison d'être. She who employs it looks pulled together but entirely natural. It is a look that says, *I have better things to do with my time than spend an hour meticulously applying my makeup! I have places to go and things to achieve. I have a life!* Yet this woman also cares how she presents herself to the world. She knows that looking mysterious but naturally beautiful adds to her charm.

I love the idea of *le no-makeup look* and wholeheartedly embrace it because before I discovered it, makeup application was a bit intimidating to me. I either wore a lot of it (for going out at night) or I didn't wear any at all; there was no in between. I never really knew how to wear makeup during the day.

So I started to experiment and to do my research. I wanted a look for every day that would subtly enhance my beauty—thereby giving me a certain polish and added confidence. I wanted the application to be quick and easy—something that I would feel confident doing every day. I wanted the look to be extremely natural—so much so that people would wonder, looking at me, if indeed I was wearing makeup. In short, I just wanted to look *great*.

I started to experiment with my daytime look while living in Paris. I tried to emulate the fresh-faced women I observed every day, and I continue to cultivate and refine the look to this very day.

Le No-Makeup Look

The following are my three favorite variations that I observed while living in Paris.

Au naturel

This look is very subtle. It includes a light foundation to even out the skin (either powder or tinted moisturizer), blush, mascara, and a neutral lip color. It is just enough to give you a pretty, professional polish but also looks completely natural. This takes almost no time to apply and is a great look for every day—for when you just want to feel pulled together. The au naturel look is perfect for professional endeavors like job interviews as well as quotidian adventures like running errands.

Defined eye

This variation features a defined eye and neutral lip. It uses the same items as the au naturel look but adds my favorite makeup product—eyeliner. This look is very gamine, very Parisian, and suggests that the wearer is more chic than the average person. She simply got out of bed, tied her hair back, slicked on some eyeliner, and went about her day! (In my case it takes a bit longer to get ready, but you do get the idea.) The defined eye look is great for visiting museums, watching films, attending casual concerts, or engaging in any artistic endeavor. Wear it when you would like to look mysterious. (Highlighting the eyes always ups the mysterious factor in a woman.)

Defined lip

This variation showcases a defined lip (red maybe?) and neutral eye. It would include powder, blush, a bold-colored lipstick (berries, mauves, or reds), and a neutral eye (no eyeshadow, just mascara, with eyeliner optional). This look is more romantic and clearly draws attention to the mouth—perfect for when you are feeling passionate, whimsical, or adventurous. It also suggests that you have better things to do than carefully apply makeup every day, but that you are feminine enough not to forget your lipstick! The defined lip is great for a first date (or any date!) or for any day that you feel like adding color to the face. In the dead of winter, it can boost your morale to use a vibrant shade (such as fuchsia) to highlight your pout.

Tailor Your No-Makeup Look to Your Outfits

When choosing your outfit for the day, you can also decide which variation of *le no-makeup look* to employ. Your makeup should be tailored to match the style of your outfit. For example, if your plans for the day consist of running errands and you are wearing a casual top, capri pants, and sandals, you could employ the au naturel look—a sweep of powder foundation, some mascara, blush, and a neutral lip color. You will feel pulled together and pleased with your appearance, especially if you run into people you know while running errands (which I *always* do). Even if you aren't planning on seeing people you know, it is nice to just look good for the sake of feeling good. I can't tell you how many times I am out in public and am inspired by the way a complete stranger looks. I often want to tell the person: You look beautiful (or handsome) and have inspired me! Be *that* person when you are running errands or are engaging in any casual activity.

If you are wearing an outfit that is a bit more playful, edgy, or artistic, the defined eye can be a great look. If you are wearing a very feminine blouse, the defined lip is great. Match your makeup looks to your outfits.

A Two-Minute Look

This look is for very casual days or when you are really pressed for time. It is the barebones version of the *au natural* look described above. The two-minute look for me consists of three things:

- concealer
- mascara
- lip color

Concealer

Most of us benefit from the use of concealer. I know I do—I have the dark circles under my eyes that plague so many of us new mothers. I also have a few tiny veins that show themselves on my right cheek and there is the occasional blemish or dark spot that needs to be covered up.

The goal of the two-minute look is to even your skin tone. I would suggest going to your favorite beauty counter and working with a professional to find the correct shade of concealer for you. If you pick a shade out on your own, you might get the color almost right, but a professional could help you pick the perfect shade—one that literally blends into your skin, rendering the concealer invisible. And the whole point of concealer is to be invisible; otherwise your problem areas become less concealed and more conspicuous!

Blend the concealer in wherever you require it. Look at your face in natural light to make sure you have blended correctly. Many times we apply our makeup according to the lighting in our bathrooms or vanities and then step outside to find we haven't blended properly for natural light.

Mascara

If you have time, curl your lashes. If you don't have time, that is okay too. Simply coat your lashes with your favorite mascara. The fewer coats, the more natural the look. I happen to like the look of mascara, so I tend do a minimum of three coats on each eye. Mascara shades and defines your eyes and is a quick way to add polish to your look. My favorite mascara is Chanel Inimitable Intense in black.

Lip color

Lip color is everything from lip balm to lip gloss to lipstick. Use what you feel like using and what you have time for. No matter what the time constraints, I always make time to moisturize my lips. Dry and cracked lips never look good. And the subtle gloss of even a colorless lip balm is enough to add a little polish to your finished look. I don't usually go for very bright colors on my lips when I'm doing the two-minute face because it seems out of place, but if you feel inspired to use a bold color—go for it!

A Five- to Ten-Minute Look

All three *le no-makeup look* variations can be achieved in five to ten minutes, it's just a matter of which one you pick. A ten-minute look usually consists of:

- concealer
- foundation
- blush
- brow color and grooming
- eyeliner (optional)
- mascara
- lip color

Concealer

See the two-minute look.

Foundation

After you have applied your concealer, sweep on your foundation to further even out your skin tone. I like to use mineral makeup, as it is sheer and light. I've also used tinted moisturizers in the past and other light liquid foundations. I would recommend going to a makeup counter and getting a professional consultation regarding which foundation is right for your skin. If you have beautiful skin or do not like to wear foundation, you can easily skip this step. I personally find it necessary to wear foundation when doing the more elaborate looks because I feel slightly undressed without it. If I am using blush and eyeliner, for example, and am not wearing foundation, I feel as though I am wearing a great top and shoes but no pants! Foundations are not what they used to be—they don't have to be cakey masks that hide your true skin. Find a sheer one that compliments your skin and brings out the beautiful colors and tones of your face. After I use foundation, I like to finish it off with a sheer dusting of translucent powder to make sure my makeup is set. My favorite foundation, which I've been using for years, is the Bare Minerals matte foundation in medium beige. I also like Hourglass Illusion tinted moisturizer in beige. Both foundations have an SPF built in.

Blush

I love blush. This is a recent thing. I never quite understood how to use it and thought if I applied it, I would look like a little girl playing dress-up. But a little pop of color on the cheeks can warm up the face and really enhance your skin tone. The key with blush is to blend it properly. You do not want to see any lines or streaks. There are so many options with blush—powder, liquid, creams, gels, and even balms. Pick a color that you love that inspires passion. After all, flushed cheeks are the very essence of passion and romance. Sweep the color on your cheeks and blend, blend, blend for the most natural of looks.

Brow color

If you have eyebrow issues (sparse, uneven, too thin, or different lengths), you could really benefit from brushing your eyebrows and filling them in with the right color. Almost every makeup brand has a product to address the eyebrows. I like to use eyebrow powder. Make sure you get exactly the right color for your brows. You don't want to go too dark (or you might look angry!) and you don't want to go too light. This is an area where you could also benefit from getting a professional's opinion. Fill in your eyebrows gently so they look full and natural.

Eyeliner

Use eyeliner (my favorite makeup product) when you want to employ the defined eye version of *le no-makeup look*. This is the look I go for the most. If the eyes are the windows to the soul, then eyeliner is like adding curtains to those windows! Before I apply eyeliner (or any eye makeup, for that matter) I always use a primer. My eyelids tend to get greasy during the day, smudging my makeup, and a primer keeps my eye makeup in place the entire day. So after I gently rub a primer on my eyelids, I apply my eyeliner. For simple definition and a natural look, most days I use brown eyeliner. As a brunette with green eyes, I find brown looks more natural on me than black. Some women wear black eyeliner and look *amazing,* but on me it can be a little harsh. Choose the right color for you, and have fun experimenting! On days when I feel a bit more bold and artistic, I use black eyeliner. Whether you use pencil, liquid, gel, or powder eyeliner, apply it with a steady hand. Practice makes perfect.

Mascara

See the two-minute look. Mascara should be applied after your eyeliner or any other eye makeup you use.

Lip color

If you are not doing the defined eye and would rather do the defined lip, pick a lip color and modality. There are many options: lipsticks, lip glosses, chubby lip pencils, colored lip balms. Even though I am defining my lips, I still like to look somewhat natural. I usually just dot lipstick on to give myself a natural, flushed look. Some of you might wish to apply lip liner and a bold color like red. Or maybe a light pink gloss is enough for you. Experiment with what suits your personality and goes with your outfit for the day. For the ladies who are of a certain age, a bold lip color can really add brightness to your complexion. I am always in awe of the beautiful French presenter Marie-Ange

Horlaville, who hosts the show *Nec Plus Ultra* on TV5Monde. She is a woman of a certain age and more stylish and beautiful than many younger presenters. Madame Horlaville always wears bright red lipstick—so glamorous and the perfect example of the defined lip variation of *le no-makeup look*. Madame Chic also wore bold lip colors—deep pinks or reds. The shock of color really brightened her face.

A Fifteen-Minute Look

This is for when you have a special event to attend or just wish to amplify your look. Requiring fifteen or twenty minutes, the look employs everything discussed in the previous looks, with the addition of eyeshadow. Generally if eyeshadow is being used, the eyes are being defined and the lip color will be neutral.

Eyeshadow

Apply eyeshadow (on top of primer) first, before any other makeup. If you get eyeshadow powder on your skin, you can easily dust it off without ruining your foundation. When used properly and tastefully, eyeshadow can really bring out the eyes and create a sexy and mysterious look. I am generally not a fan of loud colors for eyeshadow. This is still *le no-makeup look*, remember! I like to go for a natural, smoky eye. Because my eyes are green, the colors that look best on me are taupes and plums. Find the colors that you love and that look great with your eyes. If you are like me and happen to be intimidated by picking which eyeshadow shades go together, most makeup lines sell their eyeshadows in duos or quads where the shades complement each other. It also helps to have different brushes to apply each shade, but those are not entirely necessary, as you can always use the applicator that comes with most eyeshadows. The important thing to have is a blending brush. This is non-negotiable. Blending your eyeshadow well is the key to creating a natural and flattering look. And remember: before applying shadow, always prime your eyelids for longer wear.

A Word on Finishing Sprays

Finishing sprays are wonderful for *le no-makeup look* (or any makeup look, for that matter). Spritzing a finishing spray on your final makeup application can make your makeup last several hours without a single touch-up. I use a finishing spray every day—I feel my beauty routine is quite incomplete without it! Plus I no longer have to lug my makeup bag with me everywhere in case I need to do an emergency touch-up. With a finishing spray there is no need! I like Skindinävia Original makeup finishing spray, but there are several on the market. Try samples and find the best one for you.

Le Recap

- Come up with a low-maintenance no-makeup look to wear every day, and always look your best.

- Go with the au naturel look for fresh-faced beauty.

- Use the defined eye technique for a bit of natural drama.

- Wear the defined lip look when feeling whimsical or romantic.

- Tailor your application time to your schedule.

- Keep your outfits and daily activities in mind when deciding what makeup to wear.

- Consult professionals whenever possible to pick the most flattering shades for your skin tone.

- Use a finishing spray to keep your makeup in place. (Touching up your makeup in public is not chic!)

- Have fun experimenting and don't forget to change things up every now and then . . .

Chapter 7

TAKE CARE OF YOUR SKIN

While I was studying in Paris, my favorite class was art history. It was taught by someone I will call Professeur Immaculate. (This was obviously not his real name, but as with Mesdames Chic and Bohemienne, I can't resist giving him a spot-on moniker). Professeur Immaculate was a British man who had adopted Paris as his home. He was an avid observer, student, and teacher of French art and was quite possibly the most knowledgeable and interesting professor of my college career. I call him Professeur Immaculate because he had extremely high standards with regard to beauty. He was an art connoisseur, you see, and held aesthetics to be highly important.

On Mondays we would sit in the classroom and look at slides of some of the world's most famous paintings. Professeur Immaculate would tell the most fascinating stories involving drama, intrigue, and artistic license. On Wednesdays we would go to one of Paris's many illustrious museums to view the art we had studied on Monday.

One Wednesday morning as I got ready for class, I was dismayed to discover that overnight a large pimple had formed in the middle of my nose.

My entire teenage and adult life I have struggled with blemishes. They seemed to show up out of nowhere! I would get one completely without warning and it would be major—not the sort of pimple you could easily cover up and happily ignore until it went away.

I had not yet discovered the marvel that is *le no-makeup look* and did not have a concealer on hand. Now, I know the number one rule with pimples is *do not touch*—the number two rule being *lightly conceal them until they go away*. I didn't know those rules back then and poked and prodded this awful pimple with the hope that it might just go away. It did not. Instead it got bigger. And redder.

I was now running late. Our class was meeting at the Musée

d'Orsay to view Manet's *Le déjeuner sur l'herbe*, one of my favorite paintings. I wasn't going to miss that because of a silly pimple, so I decided to employ the effective tool of denial and just move on with my day.

The class was, as usual, fascinating. I loved learning about my favorite paintings and enjoyed myself immensely. When it was over, I went to ask Professeur Immaculate a question regarding a painting we had seen. I waited until another student was finished speaking with him and then walked up to pose my question. Halfway through my query I became acutely aware that Professeur Immaculate was not listening to me. He was staring at me, but not my eyes. Instead his focus lay on my nose, which I remembered, with mortification, had a large pimple on it. I meekly finished my question, and Professeur Immaculate seemed to move in to examine the pimple from a closer range. Then he said after a few moments (and after I had sufficiently withered under his gaze), "I'm terribly sorry, what was the question?"

After that day I started to notice Frenchwomen's skin—including the complexions of Madame Chic and Madame Bohemienne. They both had clear, beautiful skin. Neither of them had major wrinkles, sagging skin, sun damage, or (do I even need to say it?) pimples. Come to think of it, all my female French professors had beautiful skin too. As did the lady who worked at the local *tabac* and the one at the café . . . What was the secret to their radiant skin?

Frenchwomen are known for taking good care of their skin. And not just the skin on their faces. We've all heard about how they employ creams to combat cellulite, and keep their necks and décolleté firm. That familiar phase *bien dans sa peau* refers to beautiful skin as well as the body and soul inside it as the source of confidence and a certain ease.

Skin care is *the* most important aspect of French beauty. After all, if one is going to be comfortable in one's skin, that skin better be in top condition! Good skin is a status symbol, and thanks to the copious options available in France (facials, specialty creams, or massages), most anyone can achieve it.

L'Eau Is Key

You must drink plenty of water if you want to have good skin. Many Frenchwomen drink a tall glass of water before they go to bed and a tall one when they wake up—as well as several throughout the day. I adopted this practice after living in France. It is quite easy to go through the day and not drink enough water. If you create the ritual of drinking a tall glass before bed and one upon waking, you start the day off hydrated and reinforce the habit of continuing to drink water throughout the day.

You don't need all those frappuccinos, soy lattes, juices, and sweet teas to get you through the day. I'm not suggesting giving them all up, but make water your main beverage. (Note—this is also a technique to stay slim. All those other drinks have calories that you could do without.) Madame Chic would mainly drink water. She would have a cup of tea with her breakfast, and when she threw a dinner party, her favorite apéritif was tomato juice while the rest of us usually had whiskey (which was much more fun, I will admit, but then she had the great skin and I didn't!).

Try to cut down on alcohol consumption too—especially the sugary cocktails. Madame Chic rarely drank alcohol. She had an occasional glass of wine with dinner—but not often. By avoiding alcohol she stayed hydrated, which probably helped her skin look so young. If you are in the habit of having a glass of wine every night with dinner, try to drink a lot of water before and after to make sure you stay hydrated.

Before going to bed I like to drink a glass of water into which I've squeezed a slice of lemon. Lemon has detoxifying properties and can help settle an upset stomach. At night when I feel tempted to have a coffee, I have a hot water with lemon. I also have this at restaurants when everyone is having their espresso after their meal. The lemon helps to calm me down, and later that night I'm always grateful I didn't have caffeine!

Make sure you also eat lots of fruits and vegetables. Not only do these foods work wonders for the skin by providing antioxidants, they also contain a lot of water and are essential for hydrating the skin.

Choose Passion over Stress

It's hard to be passionate *and* stressed at the same time. The French much prefer to be passionate.

I believe most of my breakouts are due to stress (the rest to hormones). Sometimes I catch myself going through the day holding my breath or keeping tension in my shoulders. This tension cuts down my circulation, shortens my breath, and causes my skin to break out. Notice what stress does to your body—chances are it affects your skin. Do whatever you can to keep your stress levels down.

Mesdames Chic and Bohemienne did not seem stressed out at all. They both had things to be stressed about. Madame Chic, though she worked part-time, did run the entire house herself without even the occasional help of a cleaner. Cleaning the home, planning meals, shopping for them, preparing them, and doing the laundry for four people, as well as throwing dinner parties every week and working, can be stressful! (I'm getting stressed out just thinking about it.) Madame Bohemienne did all that but worked full-time *and* she was a single mother! These women were no different from all the women around the world who do these things, but they did manage to keep calm and seem less harried than most women I've observed back home.

Madame Chic combated stress with her daily brisk walk to the shops. Exercise is excellent for combating stress, and brisk walks (especially in the cold air) are actually quite good for one's complexion. She also seemed to take pleasure in every task she tackled—no matter how mundane. Madame Bohemienne did as well. She thoroughly enjoyed walking through her beloved city every day. She relaxed with a glass of wine or her famous champagne cocktail when throwing dinner parties, and viewing art in her spare time gave her enormous pleasure.

We all have different methods that work for us. To counteract stress, I like to do yoga, meditate, play the piano, go on walks, or take a hot bath with a decadently fragrant bath oil. I also get regular massages, which brings me to my next point.

The Power of Massage

Massage is an important part of taking care of one's skin. Not only does a good massage tame stress but it can also clear toxins from the body. Be sure to drink a lot of water after any bodywork to achieve the maximum benefit. Whether you get professional massages or romantic massages from your partner, try to get them regularly.

There are wonderful little foot spas all over Los Angeles that offer one-hour full-body shiatsu and reflexology massages for only twenty-five dollars. Because the price is so affordable (even with a generous tip), I try to get one once a week. Since I started getting massage regularly, I've seen a major drop in my stress levels and a major improvement in my skin. If you don't have something that affordable in your neighborhood, get creative.

Add a ten-minute massage the next time you get a manicure, or seek out a massage school near you and get one from a student at a discounted rate.

Consult Professionals

When it comes to your skin, consult professionals regularly. Dermatologists, estheticians, and other skin care professionals will guide you in solving your skin problems. I started to get regular facials once I created room for them in my budget. Getting facials on a regular basis has done wonders for my skin. The exfoliations, the peels, and the regular extractions have improved the overall quality of my skin, allowing me to not rely so heavily on makeup to cover up my imperfections.

Do your research by asking for recommendations from friends or reading reviews online, and find someone you trust. Develop a relationship with your skin care professional. My go-to person in Santa Monica is Lisa Lianna Mayer of Petite Spa. She has been taking care of my skin for years now and knows exactly what it needs. I love to sit in the tiny, serene lobby of Petite Spa, sipping on cucumber water, waiting for my facial. Then I get to lie down for an hour and be cleansed, exfoliated, massaged, and moisturized. (I've even learned to tolerate the extractions!) It is a welcome ritual that always leaves me rejuvenated.

If you can't afford frequent facials, you can do them for yourself at home. After cleansing your skin, open your pores by placing your head over a bowl of hot water infused with fragrant oils. Then exfoliate, apply a mask, remove it, and moisturize. And even though you aren't in a real spa, you can still have a relaxing experience. Lock yourself in your bedroom so no one can bother you. Play relaxing music and take deep breaths . . .

Find the Best Products for Your Budget

The French are known for spending a lot of money on skin care products. Here they do not skimp—they will buy the best creams, serums, and cleansers they can afford. And while I tend to agree that you get what you pay for with regard to skin care products, you can also find affordable drugstore alternatives as well. Be honest with your esthetician about what your skin care budget is. He or she will be able to steer you in the right direction and let you know (based on your skin needs) where you should splurge and where you should skimp. For example, if you are thirty-two years old, it might not be necessary for you to invest in an expensive neck-firming cream. You might choose instead to invest in a good antiaging eye cream. It's all about what your priorities are.

One purchase that I do recommend for everyone (and many makeup artists and beauty professionals agree!) is the Clarisonic, a sonic skin care tool. I have taken it upon myself to be the unofficial spokesperson for this miracle product. I tell everyone about it! I hesitated for a long time before I bought it because I wasn't sure I could justify the expense (it starts at around $100). Now I wish I had bought it sooner—it has transformed my skin. The Clarisonic gently exfoliates and gets rid of all the dead skin cells while allowing whatever cleansing product you use to penetrate deeper in your skin. Everyone I know who uses the Clarisonic reports a dramatic change in their skin for the better almost instantly (myself included).

Not all skin care products need be ultraexpensive. One morning in Paris the water was turned off in Famille Chic's building. Madame Chic gave me her rosewater tonic to cleanse my face since we did not have water. She swore by it and used it all the time to maintain her beautiful skin. That day my skin felt quite toned. Rosewater is a very inexpensive product; you can even make it yourself.

Protect Your Skin

In my teens and early twenties I loved to go to the beach or sit by the pool and get a suntan. My skin tans really easily and I loved the deep bronze look I could achieve with just an hour in the sun. I still love to lie out in the sun once a year on holiday (even though it is not recommended!) but I try to make up for it the rest of the year by wearing sunscreen on my face, neck, and décolleté every day—even if it's cold and cloudy outside. I always wear sun protection when sunbathing too. If you are worried about getting sunspots or wrinkles or acquiring skin cancer but you happen to spend a lot of the time in the sun, I suggest wearing a wide-brimmed hat in conjunction with high-factor SPF sunblock. I love to wear hats anyway, because they can make one look so mysterious.

And Most Important . . .

Smile, express yourself, and live passionately in your skin. Be comfortable and confident with who you are. Ignore the haters (if you have any—most people do). Take comfort in being yourself. Nothing could be more attractive.

My At-Home Skin Care Routine

My at-home skin care routine is very detailed. At times I can be a bit neurotic about it, but I have discovered that taking care of my skin is a delicate dance that must constantly be assessed in order to keep my skin in top shape.

Evening

I wear makeup almost every day (not a lot—just my ten-minute *le no-makeup look*) and it is critical that I take all my makeup off and cleanse properly every single night to avoid breakouts.

I start by removing my eye makeup very gently with eye makeup remover and two cotton squares. Then I use my Clarisonic paired with a cleanser to cleanse my skin. The Clarisonic stays on for exactly one minute and I spend the whole minute cleansing my face and neck with gentle pressure in small circular movements. Next I rinse my face with water, at room temperature or a bit warmer, and pat gently with a dry facecloth that I *use only for my face*. I find this detail to be very important. Wherever I go—whether I am at home, staying with family, or in a hotel—I always designate a towel just for my face. By doing so I can ensure that there is no shampoo, conditioner, or other residues on the towel that could clog my pores.

After I gently pat my skin dry with my face-only towel (I warned you I was neurotic), I usually apply a toner, an alpha hydroxy acid (AHA) exfoliant, and some sort of serum or vitamin C concentrate, then rub in a night cream in a gentle, upsweeping motion. These steps can vary, as I always like to change things up. Sometimes I use an exfoliating cleanser and simply apply a moisturizing serum and night cream in lieu of the toner and AHA exfoliant, and vice versa.

As for eye cream, I always gently apply it with the ring finger (it's the weakest digit and therefore the most gentle), and then I apply a lip balm to hydrate my lips while I sleep. Finally, I drink a tall glass of warm water with lemon and try to get a good night's sleep.

Once a week, on Sunday nights, I apply a face mask to banish impurities and relieve stress. My favorite face mask is the Volcanic Clay mask by Epicuren. It feels marvelously tingly. When I've had an extra stressful week, my skin actually craves it! It is also a fun ritual (even if it does scare my husband).

One of the great things about writing my blog, *The Daily Connoisseur,* is that I have the opportunity to try so many innovative skin care lines. My very favorite all-natural skin care line (which I consider to be one of my Holy Grail beauty finds) is Sibu Beauty—which uses the sea buckthorn berry as their main ingredient. I also enjoy Paula's Choice skin care products (they have great sunscreens and AHA exfoliants and mild cleansers and moisturizers), Benedetta, Dermalogica, Epicuren, and Éminence amongst others. For more in-depth reviews of my favorite skin care products, visit my blog *The Daily Connoisseur* (www.dailyconnoisseur.com).

Morning

In order to preserve its natural oils, I do not cleanse my skin in the morning. If the skin is overcleansed, it may compensate by creating too much oil, which ultimately can cause breakouts— so I leave the cleansing for nighttime. In the morning I simply splash my face and neck with warm water, then I apply a moisturizer, a sunscreen, and lip balm. After this I am ready to apply makeup.

Body

I exfoliate my skin every day by gently rubbing with an exfoliating beauty cloth or a body brush in circular motions. To cleanse my skin, I use moisturizing luxury soaps by Claus Porto, Roger &

Gallet, L'Occitane, and Diptyque, or even an organic lavender soap from Whole Foods. I use them in conjunction with my favorite bath gels. I use a body scrub twice a week. I always apply a moisturizer or body oil (or a combination of the two). During the day, I prefer something unscented or mildly scented that will not interfere with my perfume, and for evening, I love a luscious scented cream. One of my very favorite body creams is Arbordoun's Abundantly Herbal calendula cream. It's absolute magic and very healing for the skin.

When Your Skin Veers off Track

We all go through stages when our bodies change. Having babies, getting older, and going through menopause will cause your skin to change. After I had my first baby, my hormones were very erratic and my skin suffered from cystic acne. I felt so helpless, so frustrated. I was thirty years old; my skin shouldn't have been breaking out like I was a teenager!

It's important to not get stressed in these situations. That will only add to the problem. Instead I worked closely with my esthetician and dermatologist to find a solution that worked for me. I tried to keep my stress levels down and simply enjoy my newborn baby. I ate well, drank lots of water, and upped my weekly purifying mask to three times a week. It all paid off and my skin problems only lasted two months.

Since then I have discovered an acne control peel called the

Brazilian Peel Clear acne control kit that is quite effective in combating breakouts and keeping my skin on track. I use this peel and its corresponding booster pads whenever I feel like my skin might break out.

No matter what skin problems you have—wrinkles, blemishes, or age spots—it's important to remember that it is how you feel in your skin that *really* matters. Even if you find yourself being inspected by a Professeur Immaculate, remember to keep your head and just keep being you. Nine times out of ten when you think someone is looking at your imperfections, they are really thinking about their own! Most people are insecure about something. Try to put your insecurities aside and own who you are and how you look. My best advice for beautiful skin is to be comfortable in it, no matter what.

Le Recap

- Make water your main beverage of the day—limit your intake of caffeine and alcohol.

- Manage your stress levels. When you feel stress creeping up, lighten things up!

- Get regular massages from a professional masseuse or a loved one.

- Consult professionals and get regular facials if they are in your budget, or give yourself a facial at home.

- Do your research and purchase the best products you can afford.

- Protect your skin by always wearing sunscreen. And don't forget your neck, shoulders, arms, and hands!

- And most important, no matter what state your skin is in, strive to be comfortable in it. Doing so will make you most attractive.

Chapter 8

LOOK PRESENTABLE
ALWAYS

After their grand apartment, the first thing that struck me about Famille Chic was how beautifully they presented themselves. On that first day, sitting in the living room exchanging pleasantries, I noticed that Monsieur and Madame Chic were pretty dressed up, especially for a Saturday morning. I thought they might have dressed in honor of me, to welcome me to their home. But I soon learned that Famille Chic dressed up to honor no one but themselves.

Beautifully groomed and immaculately dressed, Famille Chic was a handsome family. Even their twenty-three-year-old son looked presentable always. In the six months I lived with them, they never schlepped around the house wearing sweatpants or pajamas. Madame Chic wore skirts, blouses or sweaters, and high-quality leather shoes. To leave the house she accessorized with silk scarves and a signature quilted coat. On certain occasions she donned a tailored blazer.

Monsieur Chic's casual wear consisted of trousers, pressed button-down shirts, and cashmere sweaters (he always wore a suit to work). Their son's casual wear consisted of jeans, a pressed button-down shirt, and a pullover. He always wore well-made loafers or lace-up leather shoes. I'm sure I don't even need to tell you his shirt was always tucked in and his trousers never sagging to the point of showing his underwear (an unfortunate trend among so many young men!). I never once saw any of them wearing a tee shirt the entire six months I lived with them. Save for the men's undershirts, I don't think they even owned tee shirts!

Yes, they were well dressed, but to Famille Chic, personal

presentation was about so much more than simply owning nice clothes. They were well groomed, well shod, and well mannered. In short, they exhibited themselves beautifully to the world.

Many of us (myself included) have days when we struggle to even brush our hair, pull on jeans and a tee shirt, and get out the door on time! Yet Famille Chic dealt with the same quotidian circumstances that most of us deal with. Monsieur Chic worked full-time, as did their son. Madame Chic worked part-time and took care of everything to do with the home. They were busy people! Yet looking presentable was a priority for each one of them.

Always looking presentable does not mean your appearance is "high maintenance." You wouldn't see Madame Chic running late because it took her an hour to do her makeup and flat-iron her hair. *Pas du tout.* She had her look down so well, she could put together an outfit quickly without agonizing over what to wear. She had a simple haircut that was easy to style and wore very little makeup.

Back in the days when Cary Grant and Audrey Hepburn were the most famous movie stars, everyone used to dress up— during the day, for evening, for travel, for sleeping, and even for a quick jaunt to the corner store. What happened to our society? Now it is rare to see someone nicely dressed during the day. It is more common to see men in saggy trousers with ripped hems or women in workout clothes and flip-flops. Muffin tops, bra straps, and barely covered bottoms are all on display every day. At the risk of sounding like I am ninety-five years old, *What has the world come to?*

For a long time I used the excuse of "Oh, I live in California" as a reason to walk around in sloppy tee shirts and flip-flops. I still have my moments (mainly when I'm at the playground or walking the dog at six a.m.), but now I do try to put my best foot forward, appearancewise, on a daily basis. I am not suggesting we all adopt the formalities of Famille Chic—jeans are still a big part of my wardrobe—but I do suggest that we copy their example of honoring ourselves and those we come in contact with during the day by putting some thought and effort into our appearance.

I love to watch French films. In fact, French cinema is my absolute favorite, as I find the topics and lack of commercialism to be refreshing. If you watch French films, take note of the actresses. For the most part they will look presentable always—but not too presentable. For example, in Emmanuel Mouret's *Shall We Kiss?* actress Virginie Ledoyen engages in an extramarital affair with her best male friend (played by Emmanuel Mouret). She is emotionally torn throughout the film, as she also loves her Italian husband and does not want to hurt him. Ethics aside, we still see Ledoyen going through the film looking pulled together, but not in a high-maintenance way. Her look suggests that she puts little thought into her appearance (she has a lot of other things to worry about, after all!), but even through the drama she still values the way she presents herself to the world.

So how can we all get to a place of looking presentable always?

Motivation

Avoid telling yourself you're "just going to the grocery store" (or wherever it is you happen to be going) as an excuse to look like a complete frump. You may think you won't see anyone you know—but trust me, you will. You'll see your ex-lover *and* your frenemy. We've all been in those situations where we are out in public looking less than ideal and happen to run into someone important in our lives. When this happens to me, I can barely focus on the impromptu conversation because I'm so mad at myself for looking like a schlumpadinka!

I have a mysterious neighbor who lives up the street (and whom we'll get to know better in the chapter "Cultivate an Air of Mystery"). Because I live in a town home, I have to take my dog, Gatsby, out several times a day for potty breaks (or *walkies!* as my husband calls them). *Walkies!* can occur during inconvenient moments when I happen to have just woken up or am about to go to sleep. On occasion I admit to walking the dog outside in my pajamas—which I normally try to cover up by wearing a coat. I generally aim to look presentable on *walkies!* but on the occasions when I don't (my pajamas are rolled up to my knees and I'm wearing sneakers without socks, for example), I *always, invariably, and without exception* run into my mysterious neighbor. It is an extension of Murphy's Law. It happened just the other day. I was just popping outside for ten seconds to throw out the trash in my jeans rolled up to my knees (I was doing some gardening on my balcony), gardening shoes, makeup-less face, and haphazard hair. As I was about to throw out the trash, guess who walks around the corner? My mysterious neighbor! Now I can see why Madame Chic applied lipstick and tied her silk scarf around her neck even when she was popping down to the corner store for a baguette. You never know who you'll run into.

Even if you don't see someone you know, you should want to look good for yourself. Whenever I see a well-dressed and well-groomed stranger, I am immediately intrigued. Just spotting such a person is enough to brighten my day. Every now and then in Santa Monica (the *capital* of casual wear) I see a man wearing something similar to what many Frenchmen wear—pressed button-down shirt, blazer, tailored trousers or jeans, and buttery loafers. His hair is cut, his face is shaved (or with a controlled five-o'clock shadow), and his sunglasses are on. I tell you, I swoon! Men, if you are single and want to attract the ladies, well groomed, well dressed, and well mannered is the route to take!

There is a young woman who rides her bike by my street

almost every day. She works at the local real estate office on Montana Avenue. (I know this because there is a plaque on her bicycle with the real estate office's logo.) She is always immaculately dressed—the perfect vision of business casual. She usually wears skirts paired with tailored blazers, an artfully tied scarf around her neck, and ballet flats on her feet and lets her pretty, long blond hair flow in the breeze behind her. The other day I saw her in riding pants and boots, blazer, scarf, and aviator sunglasses. She always looks fabulous! It is a joy to observe her. So if nothing else, dress for yourself and to make the world more interesting for people watchers like myself!

First Impressions

First impressions are indelible. If you are in the habit of looking presentable always, you will never need to worry about making a bad first *visual* impression. As we walk through life, we never know who we are going to meet—potential husbands or wives, coworkers, new friends. We would all like to attract the best people in our lives. If you try always to look your best, you can let go of this care and automatically feel more attractive and confident that you are making the best possible first impression.

Don't Tempt Yourself to Be Frumpy

Throw out any clothes that are overworn, damaged, or unflattering. There is no excuse for holding on to bad clothes: they serve no purpose. Even if you live alone, you shouldn't wear them. Just think, if you don't own one frumpy outfit, then you don't have to worry about ever looking frumpy!

Check Yourself from Different Angles

Before leaving the house each morning, look at yourself in the mirror from all angles. Often what can appear presentable and pulled together from the front can be a proverbial hot mess from the back. Case in point: One day as I was walking to lunch with my daughter, I spotted a woman in front of us. This woman was walking at a brisk pace. She was wearing a white tee shirt, jacket, and maroon cotton pants. She was carrying a large Louis Vuitton handbag on her right arm. Her pants were too tight around her bottom and silhouetted her cellulite as she walked. To make matters worse, there was a medium-size hole in the seam of her pants—right in the middle of the pant seat! When she turned around, I noticed her hair was styled nicely and she was wearing makeup, so this was clearly a woman who cared about her appearance. She probably had no idea of the magnitude of the wardrobe malfunction taking place on her backside. This reminded me of the woman who had the holes in the backside of her leggings. I began to wonder if I've ever walked around with a hole in *my* pants! These women could have easily avoided these fashion faux pas by looking at themselves from all angles in the mirror before they left the house.

Travel

Ladies and gentleman, let's revert to the days when people dressed up to travel. Dressing up does not equal being uncomfortable. I'm sure you know this and I am preaching to the choir. Let's spread the word, as Gandhi said, by being the change we want to see in the world. (I am quite certain Gandhi was not talking about dressing beautifully for air travel when he said that, but you do get the idea.)

You can wear comfortable travel clothes that are also chic. Black knit trousers and a dolman-sleeve top paired with ballet flats and a pashmina is an outfit that is just as comfortable as a tracksuit and tennis shoes and much more presentable. Or consider wearing a dress or skirt and bringing a cashmere wrap to keep yourself warm on the plane. For men I love jeans, a button-down shirt, and a V-neck cashmere sweater paired with suede loafers. (Can you tell I love this look?) It is a polished, respectable way to look while traveling and might even get you upgraded. (That is, if you aren't already flying in first class!)

It is possible to wear jeans and a tee shirt and look nice while traveling. Waiting in line to check in at the airport when my husband and I were coming home from Barbados last year, I spotted a woman waiting to check in to first class. She was wearing jeans (but the clean kind that were tailored and without holes in them), a tucked-in white tee shirt, very high sable nubuck Christian Louboutin heels, aviator sunglasses, and a gold watch. Her hair was brushed into a well-groomed ponytail. She was dressed casually and comfortably (with the exception of the shoes—ouch!) and managed to make jeans and a tee shirt look luxurious with her use of accessories and impeccable grooming. Also, by tucking in her pressed white tee shirt, she managed to not look frumpy. It didn't hurt that her jeans fit her perfectly too and were, I'm assuming, tailored. I'm sure once she got on the plane, she took her Louboutins off and slid on a pair of ballet flats—but then again, one never knows.

The "Saving Things for Later" Mentality

Do you have a new blouse but you haven't worn it yet because you are saving it for just the right moment? Well, if that special moment comes, by all means wear it, but in the meantime wear it to your dentist appointment too—after all, they do put a bib on you—and you might run into an old friend in the waiting room!

Sleepwear

Try not to relax your standards just because it is no longer daytime and you are not in public anymore. Whether you are a newlywed, have been married for twenty-five years, live with a roommate, or are single and have only your cat to impress, you should still look presentable in your lounge and sleepwear.

Dressing gowns are marvelous. Sadly they have become

a lost art. I love *Agatha Christie's Poirot* and especially David Suchet's portrayal of the title character. In these little period gems I am always delighted when a murder has occurred in the middle of the night and the suspects are summoned to the drawing room in their sleepwear. Beautiful dressing gowns are inevitably on display—pretty kimono-style silk numbers for the women and sturdy, quilted-lapel robes for the men. I like to collect dressing gowns and don't feel dressed if I'm not wearing one while walking around the house at night. Even if my husband is out and the children are asleep, I still wear a dressing gown to cover my pajamas.

Wearing a dressing gown, however, does not give one license to wear frumpy pajamas. I love classic button-down pajamas for men. And women? We get to have all the fun! There are options from beautiful slips to long negligees to pants and lace-trimmed chemises. Of course you could always opt to sleep naked à la Marilyn Monroe, but if you choose to do that, it is crucial to keep a dressing gown by your bed. You never know—there could be an earthquake or a fire in the middle of the night and you might end up on the street holding nothing but a pillow!

Madame Chic wore floor-length dressing gowns in pastel colors. I never actually saw her pajamas because her dressing gown covered them so well. I never saw Monsieur Chic or their son in their pajamas either. They were always dressed for the day when outside their bedrooms. Decide what is appropriate for you. I have much more to say on the subject of pajamas and what Madame Chic thought of mine, but I will save that story for the chapter "Always Use the Best Things You Have."

Hair and Grooming

It is much easier to look presentable if your hair is neat. By *neat* I do not mean pin straight or fashioned in a perfect coif; I'm talking about your signature style. Madame Bohemienne had wild, curly hair. It was trimmed regularly and she always wore it flowing free. It was her signature (along with her Bohemian skirts). I got the impression that this was not a very contrived look. She had a haircut she could style quickly and effortlessly. The same went for Madame Chic, who had a very typical short Parisian bob. Every day she wore her hair in the same style, easy and effortless. She didn't need curling iron routines, hair extensions, hairspray, or teasing. Of course these things are always fun to use on special occasions, but you free up time by not using them every day.

Find a hairstylist you love and make her your go-to person. A proper stylist will be able to give you the right cut for your hair type—one that you can easily style for effortless everyday wear. If you have dry hair like mine, it can be incredibly liberating to learn that you don't need to wash it every day. Every other day or even every third day is just fine.

In short, looking presentable always is simply a matter of respect—respect for yourself, for people you love, and for everyone who comes in contact with you.

A Word on Parisian Window Washers

Of course it can be rather difficult to look presentable always—especially if you happen to be naked and taken by surprise, as I discovered one morning in Paris. Allow me to explain . . .

I quickly got used to sharing the one bathroom in Famille Chic's apartment with the three other members of the family. On my first day, Madame Chic asked me whether I preferred to take my baths every morning or every evening. Hmm. I chose morning and secretly wondered if I would also be able to take the occasional hot bath before bedtime. I thought I might ask but decided not to push it—especially on my first day there. (As I learned later, Famille Chic was very environmentally conscious and did not like to waste water. Hence their strict policy on taking only one bath a day.)

Time passed and I quickly got used to my *salle de bain* routine. I kept a little basket in my bedroom that contained my toiletries, as counter space in the bathroom was sparse. Each morning at 7:00 a.m. I would go to the bathroom and partake of my morning ritual. The bathroom, like the kitchen, was very bare-bones. It was always sparkling clean and had very modest features—tile floors, a tiny mirror, and a freestanding sink with no counter space. There was no shower (which I found very odd, at first) but, instead, an ample-size tub with a handheld showerhead fixture.

The tub was situated in front of a very large window. The window did not have any covering on it (no blinds or curtains) because it did not look out on anything but a wall. One morning, about three months into my stay, I was in the bathtub bathing when suddenly I looked up to see a man in the window.

It was the window washer, doing his rounds. He was washing the windows for the entire building, suspended on one of those window-washing scaffolding things (at the time I was at a loss for the proper terminology and I still am). *Mon Dieu!* I shrieked and scrambled to find a cloth or towel or something to cover myself while simultaneously sitting up straight (I had been hunched over washing my feet—not the most glamorous of positions!) The window washer looked in the window and merely smiled and waved at me and carried on with his business. He did not leer and he did not stare. I wasn't sure whether I should have been relieved or insulted.

I immediately went to Madame Chic and told her about the Peeping Tom window washer. I expected her to be outraged—shocked! Instead she looked at me with an amused smile and said, "Oh yes, he's seen all of us in the bath. He only comes once a month."

Madame Chic probably sensed my utter bewilderment at

her nonchalance. She asked if I would feel more comfortable if she put up curtains in the bathroom. I thought about it for a moment and decided against it. Yes, it was weird, but perhaps my puritanical American instincts were in overdrive and I just needed to chill. I said *ça va*, no need for curtains. After all, when in Rome . . .

However, the next morning a makeshift curtain was installed for me. I have a feeling that the moment I left Paris, it was taken down.

Le Recap

- Dress presentably on a daily basis to honor yourself and those around you.

- Remember, first impressions are terribly important.

- Don't tempt yourself to be frumpy. Throw out or give away any clothes that are not up to par.

- Check yourself from all angles before leaving the house.

- Dress beautifully when you travel to raise the tone and encourage upgrades.

- Never save your best clothes for "later." Wear them today. What are you waiting for?

- Choose a haircut that is easily styled and that fits your lifestyle.

- Good grooming is imperative.

- When bathing in Paris, avoid leaving the blinds up unless you want to be admired by a Parisian window washer!

Chapter 9

PRACTICE THE ART OF FEMININITY

Before I lived in Paris, I was afraid of my femininity. I wasn't a tomboy, I liked feminine things, but I was afraid of what or who I could become if I let myself reach my full potential. My posture was bad. I didn't have a real haircut (my hair was too long—no layers), I covered my body with frumpy clothes. My tastes had not yet blossomed into those of a sophisticate.

But then something happened to me in Paris. It started as I observed Madame Chic. Her femininity didn't match my understanding of the word, which involved images of frilly dresses and high-heeled shoes. Madame Chic wore skirts, lipstick, and silk scarves every day—but her femininity was about so much more. She had excellent posture, was self-assured, and had great confidence—all things that I aspired to have.

So I started to observe Frenchwomen in general—the news-casters, the shopkeepers, the waitresses, the career professionals, the young mothers. They didn't all employ the same feminine techniques, but each celebrated her womanhood through certain aspects of her appearance.

I began to see that femininity could be enhanced by anything that made a woman feel beautiful and empowered. Suddenly a whole new world was opening up before me. I began to think about enhancing my beauty with clothing and subtle makeup and wondered what else I could do to celebrate the art of being feminine. What would happen if I unleashed all my femininity?

Of course culture influences what we see as feminine beauty. I am reporting on what I observed in France. French femininity seemed very refreshing. Frenchwomen saw American interpre-tations of femininity such as breast implants, fake nails, and hair extensions as *pas nécessaire* and instead used what nature gave them (with a few subtle enhancements, *bien sûr*).

Posture

Frenchwomen tend to have great posture. Sure there are bohe-mian types (not Madame Bohemienne, mind you) who wear berets, slouch, and smoke cigarettes, but I am not talking about those women. No, I'm talking about the average woman in France who carries herself with a certain fluid poise. Her posture is a key aspect of her femininity because she knows it gives her stature as a woman.

Having good posture can do a great deal for a person—man or woman! Good posture says you are confident, in control, and beguiling. It is not stiff and formal but wonderfully fluid—an active way of presenting yourself that exudes confidence. Carry yourself with poise, shoulders back and down, chest out (not too far out, just not caved in), and hold yourself with a certain ease.

Do you ever notice that when you observe someone with good posture, you tend to correct yours automatically? Since living in Paris, I have adopted the habit of always checking my posture. If I notice someone sitting up with poise, I automatically adjust myself. Good posture is contagious.

There are also situations that beg for good posture. For example, it is very hard to sit in a beautifully appointed room with hunched shoulders. Famille Chic's apartment was decorated quite formally. It felt almost unnatural to slouch in one of their armchairs surrounded by oriental rugs, antique furniture, and valuable paintings. Beautiful surroundings make you want to rise to the occasion.

I suggest decorating your apartment or home for good posture. Make your living spaces beautiful—ones that you would want to dress and sit up for. If you are surrounded by clutter and chaos, you are more likely to slump; our bodies tend to react to our surroundings. Observe yourself in different surroundings and take note. If you are in the lobby of the Paris Ritz Hotel, for example, you will invariably sit up straight—it would be hard not to! Conversely, if you are visiting a cluttered and untidy domicile, you might find your shoulders hunching in protest.

Once you begin to practice good posture, you start to have it no matter what your surroundings. Good posture can be extremely powerful. If you ever find yourself in a bad situation or one where you're intimidated, fix your posture. It enhances your femininity and makes a world of difference.

Perfume

I first visited France when I was eighteen years old. I spent six weeks in Cannes with my parents, as my father was working there for the summer. It was my first time in Europe and I was in a wonderland. The South of France is breathtaking—the sparkling blue of the Côte d'Azur oozed glamour and luxury. One day my parents and I took a trip to Grasse, which is the perfume-making capital of the world. We toured one of the factories and learned all about the art of making perfume and the intricacies of certain notes in a fragrance.

Before this trip to Grasse I had never thought much about perfume. I would occasionally steal spritzes of my older sister's signature scent, Trésor, but I did not have one to call my own. After that trip I became intensely interested in perfume and its aromatic effects.

I wanted to save my money and purchase a scent that I would love—one that would aromatically encapsulate all I was as a person—and one that would celebrate my femininity. But after a while I forgot about the allure of perfume. I would wear fruity body sprays and other unsophisticated scents, and years later when I went to live in Paris with Famille Chic, I still hadn't graduated to real perfume and found my signature scent.

In Paris I became accustomed to the European habit of the kiss on either cheek as a form of hello (or *bonjour,* rather). During these intimate greetings I became increasingly aware of the sort of perfume or cologne my French friends would wear. Chypres, orientals, florals . . . everyone seemed to have a signature scent!

Walking around Paris, I noted that perfume advertisements were everywhere. Perfumes and colognes were also artfully displayed in starring roles in several high-end shop windows. The French seemed to have a love affair with scent.

I hate to disappoint, but I do not know if Madame Chic wore perfume. I never got close enough to her to tell. We had a very formal relationship and we rarely (except for the first time we met and the last time we said good-bye) made personal contact. I would imagine her to wear a classic French fragrance like Guerlain's Shalimar—but that is only speculation.

When I moved back to California after living in Paris, I was newly inspired to find my signature scent. I did my research for several months—trying out samples of fragrances that intrigued me. I ended my search with Stella by Stella McCartney—a beautiful, fresh rose scent. In my research I discovered that rose is my favorite note in perfume. They are my favorite flowers (along with orchids), so I wasn't surprised. I wore Stella dutifully for several years until I decided to make a change to Bulgari's Rose Essentielle (with occasional dalliances with Jo Malone's Grapefruit cologne and Red Roses cologne). By the time you read this I could have an entirely new signature scent. I'm always on the lookout for extraordinary fragrances.

If you do not already have a signature scent you love, start to do your research. Find out what notes you love. Go to a great retailer with knowledgeable staff and tell them what sorts of fragrances you are drawn to. Hopefully they will offer you several suggestions and even give you samples to take home. Take your time and don't rush . . . Enjoy the process and find a perfume or cologne that you can fall in love with—one you would be happy to use as your aromatic calling card.

Every few years assess whether your signature scent still encapsulates who you are. We change—our tastes become more refined. After wearing Stella for so many years, I had grown slightly bored with it but still continued to wear it. It was only when I discovered that a new member of our family also wore

Stella that I decided to find something else. (In my opinion there is not room in a family for two people to have the same signature scent!) Discovering that the new family member also wore Stella was the inspiration I needed. Stella's scent (while still beautiful) was not who I was anymore—hence the move to Bulgari's Rose Essentielle.

It is a marvelous sensation to lean in to greet someone (or say good-bye) and smell their choice of fragrance. It says so much about a person. A signature scent is an intimate secret shared and provides a telling glimpse into the femininity of a woman.

Nails

I once was purchasing something in a maternity shop in America and noticed (it was hard not to) the cashier's over-the-top nails. She had long acrylics on her fingers with large three-dimensional anime characters glued to each nail! They were glittery, sparkly, and *very* distracting. This was a woman who loved her manicure. She happily tapped her talons as she rang up my purchase and gesticulated with her hands wildly. And while her manicure wasn't my cup of tea, it seemed to bring her infinite joy and was a creative way of expressing her femininity. To each her own.

I don't believe I saw any acrylic nails in France. Certainly the lady with the 3-D anime nails would have been an anomaly there. Most Frenchwomen (Mesdames Chic and Bohemienne included) have short, manicured nails that are painted in clear, neutral, or red shades.

I try to get a manicure and pedicure every two weeks. They are relatively inexpensive in America. (Not so in other parts of the world. In England I found a good mani-pedi will cost you an arm and an unpedicured foot!) If you happen to live in a place where manicures are affordable, it can be fun and relaxing to get them regularly. Or if getting your nails done is not in your budget, schedule time to give yourself a manicure at home and really make it an experience! At-home manicures are very easy to do and can be a relaxing ritual (for a tutorial check out my YouTube video "At Home Manicure").

I normally go for the natural look—short, filed nails with clear, neutral, or red polish. Find a look that's right for you. My friend Danya recently sported a "Roy Lichtenstein" manicure by nail artist Madeline Poole. On each of her tiny nails was a tribute to a Lichtenstein painting—they were miniature works of art! So whether you view your nails as mini canvases or prefer them to just be clean and filed, take pleasure in taking care of your hands on a regular basis.

Hair

Hair in France tends to be uncomplicated. A skilled blow-dry is about the most high-maintenance look a woman might get. French hair is very flirtatious—it suggests fun and spontaneity.

It says that you could jump in a pool at any given moment or that a man could run his fingers through it—if you so desired. It looks very soft and tousled. It does not say, "Stand back. Do not touch. If you do, a serious meltdown might occur!"

The haircut I observed most often while in Paris was the classic Parisian chin-length bob. Madame Chic had one, as did many other women. It is a haircut that one does not immediately associate with femininity, as it is short and can be austere. But the Parisian bob is in fact very feminine. Yes, it is a short cut, but generally it is one that moves fluidly (not stiffly). Also I can imagine that it does not take very much time to style this particular hairstyle—thereby freeing up its wearer to engage in other pursuits. I know that any amount of extra time I could find in a day would be welcome and would make me very happy. (And feeling genuinely happy does wonders for one's femininity!)

At USC one of my college French classes was taught by a Frenchwoman who had a quintessential Parisian bob. This teacher was feminine, mysterious, _French_. She always wore the simplest clothes—a colorful knit shirt or sweater paired with a plain skirt and low heels (the epitome of French minimalism). She sported _le no-makeup look_ and minimal jewelry. Her blond bob capped it all off, visually announcing that her low-maintenance look was a tribute to her natural beauty.

The Parisian bob isn't for everyone, though . . . Back in California I tried it myself in a rather spontaneous moment of optimism. My hair is very full and curly, so when I suggested the bob to my stylist, he tried to talk me out of it, but nothing could deter me! I wanted an effortless, chic Parisian bob—one that would free up the time I spent styling my hair. Something that could become my signature look! But unfortunately, with my wild curls that tended to frizz, my hair took on a curious mushroom shape and was, in two words, highly unflattering. Even though it didn't work out for me, if the classic Parisian bob is something that interests you, go for it! I am still glad I tried it, because if I hadn't, I would have always wondered . . . If you try it, I hope you will have more success than I did.

The second most popular style I saw in France was shoulder-length, soft, feminine hair—worn either curly or straight. Frenchwomen rarely go for really long hair—probably because long hair can require more maintenance. (Two of my good friends in Santa Monica, Bex and Amelia, have exquisitely long locks. Their hair is in top condition—it enchants! If my hair looked that good, I would wear it long too.)

I found the simplicity of French hair to be refreshing. I am used to seeing hair extensions, crazy cuts, and overstyled coifs, but the natural look seems much more feminine. Madame Bohemienne had curly hair that fell to just above her shoulders. It was wild and effortless and suited her personality—its natural beauty was an effective part of her feminine arsenal.

Now I have fun experimenting with my look. My hair,

though curly, tends to blow-dry quite nicely. Therefore I either wear my hair curly or make a good blow-dry last up to three days. On days I don't want to wear my hair down, I employ an easy updo—either a sleek ponytail, a top bun (very au courant), or half the hair pulled back in a clip. For special occasions I go for dramatic curls (done with a large-barrel curling iron) or Old Hollywood wavy hair à la Veronica Lake.

Whatever you decide to do with your hair—whether it is a carefree, easy style like the Parisian bob or a more high-maintenance look, make sure that it is a look that makes you happy and one you can realistically achieve easily. There is nothing worse than being a slave to one's hair. Find the perfect style for you—a signature look, perhaps, one that frees you up to enjoy your day and your many other pursuits, with your great hair as the ultimate feminine accessory.

The Case Against Overdoing It

I am always impressed by French newscasters. You must watch a French TV channel (such as TV5Monde) to see what I mean. Those women ooze femininity! They aren't showing lots of cleavage or too much leg (*Ahem,* certain newscasters in L.A.) but instead are wearing *le no-makeup look,* have soft, flowing hair; minimal, tasteful jewelry; and simple, feminine clothing. For example, one might be wearing a lilac cashmere sweater, a simple gold necklace, plum lipstick, and flowing hair. The newscaster isn't the star or the focus—the news is. Her simplicity gives her authority, *non*?

We are all familiar with the *Real Housewives* television franchise. These women definitely overdo it with their big hair, big bling, complicated clothing, and *very* high-maintenance looks. They are so overstyled that their femininity is hidden behind a web of products, labels, and plastic surgery. I'm not the only one who has noticed this. The American actress Jennifer Aniston recently abandoned her signature long locks and went for a very French shoulder-length cut to avoid (as her stylist put it) "looking like a Real Housewife."

I believe overadornment or overdoing it takes away from the woman herself. This is why I tend to appreciate more minimalist styles. I would rather see the woman than her over-the-top outfit, outrageous hair, neon eyeshadow, and costume jewelry. Your outfit should not be wearing you; you should be wearing your outfit. If you are accustomed to overadorning yourself, toning it down a bit might make you feel a tad naked. With less makeup, simple hair, minimal, tasteful jewelry, you, the woman, will be more on display. This will allow the intangible nature of your femininity to show through—which brings me to my next point . . .

Intangibles

We have discussed the visible, tangible aspects of femininity, but I believe the intangible aspects of femininity are the most important. Self-confidence, a sense of humor, a willingness to play and be adventuresome—these are all the foundations of that je ne sais quoi that so many women aspire to. You can visit the best salons, have the most expensive clothes and most polished nails, but if you do not have self-confidence to go with them, they are worth nothing.

In Paris I started to shed the various layers of self-consciousness that veiled my life. I realized that I tied my hair back all too much. That my winter coat was too bulky and shapeless and didn't celebrate the form of my body. That I avoided eye contact with interesting strangers for fear of what might happen. That I was uncomfortable having a close conversation with someone in daylight for fear my skin imperfections would be apparent. I became aware of all these things that were holding me back from being a magnificent woman.

So one brisk day in Paris as I walked from the metro in the Eleventh Arrondissement to my classes, I allowed my long, curly hair to flow down my shoulders and my lips to part ever so slightly as they wore a brand-new lip gloss I purchased at Printemps. I felt a lightness in my step as I made a conscious effort to stop hiding the real me—to shed my self-consciousness with every step I took. As I walked, I spotted a handsome, well-dressed stranger ahead of me, standing on the corner about to cross. We caught each other's eye. I smiled at him as I approached and then I paused about a foot away from him as we looked at each other. It was an intense stare and I was fully in the moment. He smiled kindly and said to me with admiration, *"Superbe."* I smiled, said nothing, and continued walking with the happy knowledge that finally my inner feelings were showing, because that handsome stranger hit the nail on the head—I did indeed feel . . . superb.

Le Recap

- Cultivate good posture and constantly check yourself until it comes naturally to you.

- Explore the world of perfume and either choose a signature scent or a capsule perfume wardrobe. Delight in the process, as perfume is one of the great joys in life!

- Strive to always have well-groomed nails— whether they are just buffed and filed or elaborately polished.

- Healthy hair in an attractive style does wonders for femininity.

- The intangible aspects of femininity, like self-confidence and a sense of humor and adventure, are the most important. Never lose sight of these things.

Part 3

How to
Live Well

Chapter 10

ALWAYS USE THE BEST
THINGS YOU HAVE

I have already described what happened my first night in the house when Madame Chic caught me sneaking off to the kitchen to grab a nighttime snack. She also gave a funny look to my pajamas, but it wasn't until a week later that she confronted me about them.

The pajamas in question were a comfortable old pair of white sweatpants and a tee shirt—my favorite combination for sleepwear. The sweats were soft from innumerable washes, and my old college tee shirt made me feel at home. So a week later as I ventured to the *salle de bain* in my pajamas, Madame Chic stopped me. The look on her face was one of concern.

"Jennifer," she said, "did I do that in the laundry?"

By *that* she was referring to the hole in the knee of my sweatpants. (Oh, yes, I forgot to mention there was a hole, didn't I?)

"Oh no," I exclaimed, eager to ease her mind, "these have had a hole in the knee for ages!"

The look of concern on Madame Chic's face grew to one of confusion. "Why would you keep them if they have a hole in the knee?" she asked.

I remember looking at her, in her chic kimono-style dressing gown, her hair pulled gently back from her face. "That's a good question," I said with embarrassment. "I don't know."

And the truth was, I didn't know. Why did I haul my ratty old holey sweatpants all the way from California to Paris (*Paris!*) to wear as sleepwear? Yes, they were comfortable, but they weren't *that* comfortable. Instantly, I felt a combination of self-consciousness, horror, and enlightenment.

I looked at my old sweatpants with fresh eyes. They didn't seem so comfortable anymore. In fact, they just seemed *sad.* I regarded Madame Chic again in her elaborate robe and slippered feet. She would never dream of holding on to such a garment that had passed its prime, let alone traveling with it or wearing it in someone else's house. Perhaps I needed to become more discerning.

That afternoon I headed straight to Etam and bought two pairs of suitable pajamas—a cream-colored button-down pajama set and a pretty orange lace chemise. The white holey sweatpants were thrown in the trash.

Later that evening I wore my new cream button-down pajamas to bed. They were not expensive but were the nicest pajamas I had ever owned because they were actually meant to be pajamas. In the past I had always worn old sweats and oversized school tee shirts to bed because pajamas were a throwaway concept to me—any old thing would do. It felt good to actually wear something lovely—that was designed with the very purpose of being slept in.

The best part was my new pajamas were just as comfortable as my old sweatpants. They were my best, and it felt luxurious to wear them on a nightly basis. This was the first time I respected myself enough to realize I deserved to wear beautiful and feminine articles of clothing at all times—not just during the day or on special occasions.

Famille Chic looked presentable from the moment they woke to the moment they went to bed (in their presentable pajamas). But what about what they wore under their clothes? For politeness' sake I will not describe their underpinnings, but I will tell you a story about mine . . .

One morning, a few days after I'd arrived in Paris, Madame Chic asked me if I had any laundry that needed washing. It was in the morning, before I went to school. When I got home, my clothes were folded neatly on my bed but my underwear was missing from the pile. I checked in my wardrobe, but the items weren't there either. Puzzled, I made a note to ask Madame Chic as to their whereabouts when I next saw her. That night was also the evening of my first dinner party with the family. I rushed to get ready as I heard a knock on the door. In a timely manner I stepped out of my room to greet our dinner party guests (a stylish, older couple) and be introduced. As we made our way to the living room for our apéritifs, I had the strange suspicion that my misplaced underpants were somewhere near at hand and looked up in horror to see them hanging on drying racks suspended from the hallway ceiling directly in front of us! I didn't know it at the time, but because French underwear tends to be delicate and of high quality, Madame Chic was in the habit of hanging her panties to dry rather than placing them in the tumble dryer.

Unfortunately I had rather unsophisticated panties in bright colors with immature slogans on them, such as *Drama Queen!* and *No Chance!* I cursed myself at the time for possessing such ridiculous items and vowed to seek out more sophisticated articles in the future. Thankfully the ceilings chez Famille Chic were very high and the hallway to the kitchen relatively dark, so I don't believe the guests saw my artless underpinnings . . .

Famille Chic's philosophy of using the best they had didn't end with clothing and undergarments. As you will see, they applied the philosophy to every aspect of their lives.

À la Table

Many of us receive presents such as crystal glasses or china for our weddings or anniversaries. In most homes, these things collect dust in a cabinet and are only pulled out twice a year, perhaps at Easter and Christmas. Our meals on the other 363 days of the year are served on chipped plates and in mismatched glasses. Please tell me I'm not the only one who sees the tragedy in this.

Famille Chic used their best for every meal. Every evening the table was set with their good china and crystal tumblers. They didn't have a separate set of wineglasses for special occasion dinners—it was crystal or nothing. In their minds, they themselves were special enough. Setting the table with their best elevated what would otherwise be a mundane quotidian experience. It made the everyday special and luxurious.

Special occasions

Some might argue that if you use your best dinnerware every day, special occasions become no longer special. To solve this problem, change something significant on the special day. Use your grandmother's delicate tablecloth, bring out the soup tureen that doesn't usually see the light of day, or go over the top with a spectacular floral arrangement.

The Home

We have all been to homes with a museum room—an untouched room where everything is in place and the family's best is displayed. This room is often off limits to family members—allowing the glory of all its wares to remain unsullied. The trouble with museum rooms is that we end up never going in them and then our best is never used!

Every piece of furniture in Famille Chic's Parisian apartment was their best. They didn't have one room with antique chairs and another room with the family sofa that is there for the dog and the kids to spill things on. No, we sat in their antique upholstered chairs, enjoying their formidable artwork on the walls, their best Persian rugs under our feet, while we sipped our apéritifs out of their best crystal tumblers—*every day*. Their best furniture gave a decidedly decadent feel to everyday life and affected everything from my posture to the way I dressed to the way I spoke.

Keep Only the Best Things You Have

We can use the example of my holey sweatpants for this one. Madame Chic would never even wear such a garment. She would have gotten rid of it the minute it was past its prime (although I must say she would never own a pair of sweatpants in the first place).

Much as you reviewed your wardrobe, go through your home with a critical eye. Become an editor. Don't even tempt yourself to use anything that's less than your best. Avoid that oh-so-common malady of "saving your best for later." As we all know, "later" rarely comes!

The Best You Can Afford

After reading this chapter, it might be tempting to throw out everything you have and go on a shopping spree. This is *not* the message I wish to convey. If you do go shopping, it is important to remember that your best must be what you can afford. It is always wise to purchase the best we can afford. Quality is always a better investment. But your best could be anything from Grandma's hand-me-down sofa—reupholstered and with new cushions—to a full set of matching plates found at a garage sale. I am not advocating that we all go out and buy Hermès china for everyday use (although that would be nice). If Hermès plates are in your budget, lucky you! If they are not, that is okay too. You can find quality wares in any price range. It just takes research and a discerning eye. The good news is that once you become accustomed to using your best, you train your eye to seek out only quality.

Manners

Famille Chic had impeccable manners and used them on a daily basis. They applied the "use your best" philosophy to their behavior toward their guests, of course, but also to their behavior toward each other every day.

Many of us use our best manners in public or when we have guests, but when we are with our immediate family members, our kindness and good manners go out the window. For example, if you are at one corner of the house and you wish to speak to your spouse, who is at the other corner of the house, you might be tempted to yell his name at the top of your lungs to avoid having to go and get him in person. I will admit, I feel like doing this all the time. We live in a multilevel town home and it can be very tiresome if I'm on the bottom floor and want to communicate with someone on the top floor. Whenever I choose to abandon my manners and yell, I instantly regret my unsavory behavior. I'm happier when I get some exercise and scale the four flights of stairs to ask for what I need in person.

What about when we are met with rudeness from strangers or, even worse, people we know? I have a rude neighbor I frequently run into, as we both have dogs to walk. Every time I see her, she says something that disturbs me (I don't think she can help it). My knee-jerk instinct is to be rude back. For instance, if she insults my dog because he growls at her, I long to say, "He is growling at you because he is a good judge of character." But instead I try to employ my best manners, excuse myself, and simply walk in the other direction. Inevitably, the next time I see her, I am glad I used manners rather than catering to my baser instincts by retaliating. In the long run, using your best manners provides the most satisfaction.

Practice Your Best

My favorite column is Sir David Tang's Agony Uncle in the *Financial Times* weekend House & Home section. In this column

Mr. Tang provides advice on the subject of "property, interiors, etiquette, home, parties and anything else that might be bothering you." One week a gentleman wrote to complain that his girlfriend did not care about how the Saturday morning breakfast table was set unless company was present. Said girlfriend claimed that to care about such things without company present was "petit bourgeois." Mr. Tang's response was right in keeping with the philosophy of using only the best things you have. He advised the writer of the query to always practice his best, especially when alone. And that by doing so they would not come across as phony when joined by the proverbial Joneses.

Develop a Taste for the Best

Celebrate everyday life by using your best. Hold your possessions and your actions to the highest of standards. Doing so can make the mundane special and life so much more interesting.

Le Recap

- Avoid saving your best for later. Use the best you have every day.

- Elevate mealtimes by using your best dishes, glasses, napkins, and tablecloths.

- Arrange a special floral bouquet or cook a fancy dish to mark special occasions.

- Use the best rooms in your home and avoid saving them for special occasions or certain guests. You deserve to use the best parts of your home every day!

- Clear out and declutter your home, and keep only the best things you have.

- When making purchases, buy the best you can afford. Always take your budget into consideration to avoid living beyond your means.

- Use your best manners on a daily basis, especially with those closest to you.

- Practice the art of living well every day—even when you are alone. Doing so allows you to develop a taste for fine living.

Chapter 11

LIVE LIFE AS
A FORMAL AFFAIR

My life in Southern California was very different from the formal life I lived in Paris with Famille Chic. In the beginning I was very thrown off by their customs. They lived like people in a period drama. Everything about them was formal—their apartment, their clothes, their manners, their meals, even their music! And while initially I felt a bit out of my element with them, their formality ultimately entranced me.

Our society has become *way* too casual. Formality is nearly extinct. And while Parisian life tends to be more traditional than the Californian life I was used to, the formality of Famille Chic was unique, a part of their aristocratic heritage. They had tradition in their veins.

Chaotic versus Formal

When we live without structure and protocol, we break rules, ignore traditions, and lack manners. Anything goes. Meals are not at set times. The television is always on in the background. Guests have to fend for themselves ("You know where the drinks are, don't you? Help yourself!") There is an element of chaos in an overly casual household. You never know what to expect.

Living formally is about honoring traditions. It is about leading a structured life and observing protocol. Formalizing everyday rituals strengthens their importance. Mealtimes are regular, proper etiquette is observed, and guests are made to feel welcome. Family dinners become meaningful. Memories are created.

Famille Chic's daily life was very structured. I always knew what to expect, and that was not a bad thing. Once I became acquainted with their routines, I knew how to fit harmoniously into their household.

For example, meals were served at the same time every day. Being able to rely on that consistency was nice. During meals, people weren't getting up out of their chairs, checking their cell phones, or watching TV. We knew that for those forty-five minutes we would be connecting and bonding over food and conversation with no distractions.

Formal interiors

The interior of Famille Chic's Sixteenth Arrondissement apartment was decorated for a formal life.

On their entryway walls hung rather formidable portraits of people who looked as though they could be Famille Chic's ancestors. These portraits in gilded frames would fit right in at the Louvre, and they let you know from the moment you walked in, this wasn't your average family.

Famille Chic's living room was decorated for socializing, not lounging. The seating consisted of upholstered armchairs facing inward to promote conversation, and their tiny television was far from the main focus of the room. Their antique record player, on which they loved to play classical music, provided the nightly entertainment after dinner.

The dining room table, when dressed for dinner, wore a tablecloth. Their dishes were blue-willow-patterned china and for glasses they used crystal tumblers. The dining room table most always displayed a fresh bouquet of flowers, artfully arranged by Madame Chic. Wine was decanted into crystal tumblers and freshly pressed coffee was sipped out of delicate blue-and-white teacups.

Famille Chic's home was beautifully appointed, but nothing was sparkly and new. Everything had a comfortable, used feel to it. The daily use of these things made the atmosphere of their home quite formal. There was no clutter (which I will discuss in the next chapter); the spareness heightened the air of formality. And despite all their traditional furniture, Famille Chic's home did not have the unapproachable feel of a museum to it.

Wardrobe

Famille Chic always dressed well. They didn't just dress nicely for the public and once home change into sweatsuits or pajamas. Their wardrobe was formal always and they were very comfortable indeed.

Most people tend to have two sets of clothes, one for public and one for the home. The clothes for public tend to be presentable and the clothes for home tend to be ratty. We might become accustomed to changing into baggy sweats the minute we get home from work, for example, in order to unwind. But is this really necessary? What would happen if we decided to remain presentable at home? Wearing nice clothing around the house affects your attitude in surprising ways. You might be more inclined to enjoy a formal meal at the dining table rather than a casual one on the sofa. Or you might be inspired to open your home to friends and entertain.

Mealtimes

Mealtimes weren't just for satisfying hunger chez Famille Chic. Mealtimes were an event. These events were imbued with a sense of ritual that had been the family's tradition for generations. For example, every evening, Famille Chic insisted on serving me first, as I was the female guest of honor. Then Madame Chic was served, then her husband, and then their son. At first, I felt awkward and protested the focus of attention conferred upon me during this nightly ritual. But once I realized they weren't putting on airs for me and that was their "normal," I saw I should respect their custom by participating in it. Everyone came to dinner promptly, waiting in the dining room while Madame Chic rolled in a cart bearing the serving dishes. Then she took her place at the table and served each of our plates. Meals would always be a minimum of three courses—usually an appetizer, main course, and dessert and/or cheese course.

You might think that the formal protocol of our meals chez Famille Chic was dictated by the older inhabitants of the house, Monsieur and Madame Chic, but that was not the case. One evening when Monsieur and Madame Chic attended a dinner party, I had dinner with three of their sons—the one who lived with us as well as his two older brothers, who lived elsewhere in the city. I thought we would have a casual meal—perhaps serving ourselves in the kitchen and sitting around the table and eating, family style. But they followed the same protocol used when the "adults" were present. In fact, the dinner was almost *more* formal. Because the two older brothers were visiting, our dinner took on the air of a dinner party. We had whiskey as an apéritif in the living room. Then we moved to the dinner table for a three-course dinner Madame Chic had prepared that consisted of prosciutto salad, tomato tart, and a cheese course. They insisted on serving me first as the female guest of honor. After dinner the boys made espressos and we adjourned to the living room to continue our conversation. The whole experience was delightfully civilized.

I laugh to think about what would have happened if my sister and cousins and I had been left unattended at that age by the adults. We probably would have ordered a pizza and thrown a house party! I have to say I prefer the formality of the brothers. I enjoyed a memorable and lovely evening with them and felt very special indeed.

How to Practice the Art of the Ritual

You can make aspects of your life more formal by practicing the art of the ritual. Famille Chic's daily life seemed to consist of one ritual after another—from how they took their breakfast to the playing of classical music on the record player after every dinner. Create luxurious rituals for yourself and your family to elevate your experience of just living to fine living. You could take a cue from Famille Chic and play music after dinner while you enjoy your after-dinner coffee or digestif. Or you could create a new tradition for your family. Perhaps the whole family could get dressed up for dinner on Saturday nights (even the kids!), or maybe you could play chess in front of the fire on Friday nights rather than watching television.

Manners

Minding manners and practicing social etiquette is (unfortunately) a dying art form. As society becomes more and more casual, we are abandoning time-honored social customs. By practicing impeccable manners, you distinguish yourself from the increasing number of people that, well . . . don't.

You may feel awkward practicing certain customs that feel dated, but honestly this is a revolution that needs to happen. People will admire you for your impeccable manners. There are certain customs of etiquette that might seem very formal but can make the world a more pleasurable place to live. Handwriting correspondences, greeting people by their formal names, opening the door for others, speaking with discretion—these are all wonderful customs to revive. Just remember always to be gracious, take the high road if met with rude people, and mind your manners.

Additionally, treating everyone you meet during the day with respect is an important aspect of living a formal life. It may seem formal to give a brief nod of recognition and a "good morning" to everyone you see while walking the dog, but once you get used to it, it can feel quite good.

I am also a huge advocate of greeting a person before speaking to them. This especially goes for service people. In France you absolutely must greet a store employee with a *bonjour* before ordering or asking a question. Omit the greeting and you will be met with a very frosty reception.

When dining alone

Practicing the art of the ritual at the breakfast, lunch, or dinner table even when eating alone may initially feel stuffy and point-less, but you'll soon see that it has many benefits. Taking your time to eat, using cloth napkins, sitting up straight, and observing your manners can help you stay slim (by helping you to focus on your food and not overeat) and prevent you from coming across as false or forced when you are joined by other people. But most important, it helps make formal living a habit.

Sushi Roku is one of my favorite places to dine in Santa Monica. Situated on Ocean Avenue, it has a front room with a beautiful view of the sea, and the food is absolutely scrumptious. One night when dining there with my husband, I observed a woman, dressed to the nines, take a table for one in the busy front room. She was wearing a form-fitting cocktail dress, and her long hair was styled beautifully and flowing down her back. She sat by herself surrounded by the hustle and bustle of a popular restaurant on a Friday evening. She didn't bring a book or check her BlackBerry every few minutes or display any of the signs of self-consciousness that one would expect from a person who is dining alone. Instead, she sat, with beautiful posture, and proceeded to order a rather lavish feast, enjoying her sushi, sashimi, and cocktails thoroughly. She even ordered dessert! When she was finished and had paid for her meal, she stood up elegantly, thanked the waiter, and glided out of the room. I'll never forget this woman, who clearly enjoyed her life and appreciated the formal aspects of dining out—even when alone.

If you feel anxious about displaying formal manners at the dinner table, simply check your self-consciousness at the door along with your coat. Displaying proper table etiquette is always the best option. If you are dining with people who do not have manners, perhaps they will catch on—after all, good manners are not only formal, but contagious.

Attire

I firmly believe it is better to be overdressed than underdressed in any situation. Any uncomfortable feeling I may get when I'm dressed more formally than others pales in comparison to the feeling I get when it is apparent that I haven't put quite as much effort into my appearance as others have.

There are certain occasions that always warrant dressing up, like any gathering where you are honoring someone or where others went to a lot of effort for your sake (for example, a performance such as a play). I can't tell you how many baby or bridal showers I've been to where I see inappropriate clothing choices.

Like jeans. Don't get me wrong, I love jeans and wear them all the time, but so does the rest of the world, and that is exactly why they should not be worn on special occasions. At least the majority of the guests I've seen wearing jeans *try* to dress their jeans up with nice jewelry and a sweater or jacket, but I'm not kidding when I say I've seen guests wear gym shoes, jeans, and a tee shirt! An outfit I wouldn't even wear to work out in! (Sorry to be so shrill, but such a blatant lack of respect and manners exasperates me.) A baby or bridal shower is an occasion where you are honoring someone—whether it is the mother and her baby or the bride-to-be. Such occasions are perfect chances to celebrate ritual and formality. Dress accordingly and wear something special.

It is *never* appropriate to wear shorts, flip-flops, sneakers, or casual (ripped, frayed, or dingy-looking) jeans to the theatre. I will go out on a precarious limb right here by saying that it is okay to wear jeans to certain more casual theatrical productions such as improv shows or spoken-word performances. Make sure the jeans fit you well, are either black or in a dark wash, and are dressed up with heels or boots and topped off with something special like a velvet blazer. Whatever you do, think dressy. Last year my good friend Newton and I attended a show at the Los Angeles Theatre Center. He wore dark jeans, lace-up leather shoes, a button-down shirt, and a gray vest and looked absolutely fabulous (not to mention appropriate), so it can be done!

Get in the habit of dressing up. Start by dressing up for dinner in the evening. I love watching films and television shows in which the characters dress up for dinner (*Agatha Christie's Poirot* comes to mind. So does *Mapp & Lucia*). What fun! To be beautifully dressed for everything from traveling on an airplane to attending the opera will help you to live a more refined and formal life.

You may be wondering if Famille Chic ever let their hair down, so to speak, and wandered around the house in their pajamas. Well, the answer to that question is *non,* but I do have a little anecdote about how Monsieur Chic let loose. Toward the end of my stay with Famille Chic, my cousin Kristy came to visit me from America. One Sunday afternoon, she and I planned to venture out and explore the city. Monsieur Chic was the only one at home. He was smoking his pipe and watching a news program on TV (a very rare occurrence chez Famille Chic). We said good-bye to him and were on our way. Halfway down the stairs I realized I had forgotten my sunglasses, so my cousin and I went back up to the apartment to retrieve them. When we walked back into the apartment, we found Monsieur Chic where we left him, smoking his pipe, but now his shirt was untucked and his feet were propped up on a footstool. When he saw us walking through the door, he rapidly sat up and tucked in his shirt—the whole while apologizing. Feeling guilty about walking in on him when his guard was down, I got my sunglasses, apologized for startling him, and left again.

On the other side of the door my cousin and I just looked at each other and smiled. Monsieur Chic's gentlemanly nature was charming.

More Ideas on How to Make Your Life a Formal Affair

Music

If you aren't already familiar with classical music, give it a try. Purchase a few compilation albums on iTunes and play them in the background as you go about your day. Such music has a way of making whatever you do feel more important. My favorite ritual of Famille Chic's was the playing of classical music after dinner every night on the record player. It made me feel like I was in a period film and I loved it.

You might love classical music but feel silly or pretentious playing it when you have guests. To that I say it is your home and you set the tone for the gathering. I don't think I've ever been to anyone's home where classical music was playing (other than that of Famille Chic, of course). I would be thrilled to hear it at a dinner party! If you are still shy, ease your way into it. Play a conversation piece that will get your guests talking. I am a big fan of the San Francisco Saxophone Quartet. They play beautiful classical music, and when you listen to them, it isn't immediately apparent that you are not listening to traditional quartet instruments like oboes, trumpets, violins, and French horns. Of course music connoisseurs would be able to tell, but even they might be thrown off.

The lost art of letter writing

Every now and then, write a letter instead of sending an email. When recently staying at my parents' home, I sorted through a box of memorabilia in my old room. I came across dozens of letters my cousin and I wrote to each other while growing up. It was so much fun to read through these letters again. At one point I laughed so hard I cried, remembering how silly we used to be! I started to get sad that we don't write letters anymore. Now our correspondences are floating around in the vast sea of cyberspace.

Letter writing is a lost art. Spoil yourself by purchasing nice thick stationery—perhaps bearing your name or initials (this also makes an excellent present). Send a letter to a loved one for no reason. Mail can be so depressing these days—usually just bills, credit card offers, or coupons. Think how pleasantly surprised the recipient of a nice, juicy formal letter would be!

Language

Learn a new word every day and incorporate it into a conversation. For example, as I write this, the word of the day on my Internet homepage is _confute_—a verb that means _to overwhelm by argument_. I challenge you to _confute_ me when I say that our society has become too casual!

Not only has language become too casual with the widespread use of slang, but it has also gotten very dirty. Don't get me wrong, certain words have always been dirty. I am just noticing that bad words are said much more freely in public than they used to be. I've been in several stores recently where I've even heard staff members curse. So not appropriate! Of course I am not claiming that I never curse. On certain occasions certain words just have to be said (like when I stub my toe), but I do try to keep it clean, more often than not. If you have the urge to curse, try to at least be creative with your outbursts. Try the following words instead: *bother, blasted, confounded,* or *dastardly.*

A Final Word

You must decide what living life as a formal affair means to you. I am not suggesting that we all stop wearing jeans, watching television, and listening to hip-hop. Not at all! What I am suggesting is that we analyze the aspects of our life that could use a little more flair. That by introducing aspects often thought of as "formal" into our lives, we can live a richer existence and pass along a lot of good habits to our children and to the people who come in contact with us.

Le Recap

- To live well, add as many formal aspects into your life as you desire.

- Create formal rituals and traditions for your family that will enrich everyday life.

- Mind your manners and take the high road always.

- Practice formal etiquette, even when dining alone, to make mealtime special.

- Dress appropriately for every occasion and remember it is better to be overdressed than underdressed.

- Cultivate your love of classical music and listen to it throughout your day.

- Write more letters. Think how thrilled the recipient will be!

- Boost your vocabulary by incorporating new words into your speech to avoid becoming too casual in your language.

- Determine what living life as a formal affair means to you and your family, and delight in it!

Chapter 12

CLUTTER IS SO
NOT CHIC

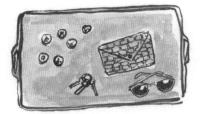

do not exaggerate when I say Famille Chic's home was completely clutter-free.

There was no pile of mail waiting to be sorted through on the kitchen table. There was no accumulation of shoes and coats by the entryway door. There were no old receipts, takeout menus, or errant coins scattered about on the coffee table. Monsieur Chic's slippers weren't lying in the middle of the hallway.

Everything had a place, and the entire time I lived with them I never saw anything out of place. Perhaps it was because of the formidable portraits of their ancestors hanging in the hallway—seeming to judge you as you walked through the door.

I probably wouldn't lay a pile of junk mail under those austere faces either! Or maybe it was because Famille Chic loved to live well, and living in constant clutter is the antithesis of living well. After all, clutter is so not chic.

What Constitutes Clutter?

One definition of clutter is anything in your home that you don't absolutely love. Perhaps you received a gift from a loved one that doesn't go with the décor of your home. You don't actually like the item but hesitate to get rid of it lest you hurt your loved one's feelings. Or maybe you are holding on to something for sentimental reasons even though you know deep down you could probably do without it. These things are clutter. Clutter is also an accumulation of miscellaneous things that do not belong where they currently are. Keys, cell phone, and wallet in the middle of the dining room table are clutter. A pile of unsorted mail on the piano is clutter. Generally you know what clutter is. You know because to look at it aggravates you.

Having said that, I firmly believe a home should not be stripped bare of character in the pursuit of banning clutter. I do not categorize as clutter collectibles or treasured items. Your beloved collection of flow blue plates on display in your dining room, for example, is not clutter. Although do be honest with yourself. If you collect things for the sake of having collections, you could have a clutter issue. A teacup, coin, toy soldier, and troll doll collection, for example, might be overdoing it a bit, more clutter than collection. Perhaps the troll dolls could be given away to a troll enthusiast? Always prioritize.

Go Slowly

Decide which areas of your home need decluttering. As you did when you cleared out your wardrobe, go slowly and do not take on more than you can handle in a given session. There is nothing worse than having lofty ambitions, pulling out the contents of an entire closet, and realizing a half hour later that you would like to be done for the day but have only sifted through a third of your mess. Be realistic and realize that accomplishing one small task a day (be it one junk drawer, one pile of filing, or one section of the closet) can boost your morale and help you remain enthusiastic about tackling the next day's task.

Reject Consumerism

Cut way down on how much you bring into your home. We do not need to buy as much stuff as we do. Famille Chic were not big consumers. They were not constantly buying things and bringing them into the home; therefore, they had less stuff to manage and ultimately find a place for. This concept will be explored in greater detail in the chapter "Reject the New Materialism."

Train Other People

Madame Chic did the majority of the housework and did not employ a cleaner. Having said that, however, she was also never running around like a maniac picking up after the members of her family. She was the most calm and collected housewife I have ever seen. This could mainly be owing to the fact that the men of the house were very respectful of the home and did not leave a mess. Monsieur Chic and their son always picked up after themselves. I have a feeling that Madame Chic trained them in the art of maintaining a clutter-free home. They simply didn't leave stuff everywhere—or *anywhere,* for that matter.

Of course, managing clutter would be a lot easier if we just lived alone and followed our own clutter management system. But then we might get lonely and life would be no fun. So we need to figure out a way to live harmoniously with our husbands or wives, children, pets, or roommates without becoming a clutter-controlling tyrant.

So how does one "train" members of the family without coming across as bossy, neurotic, or nagging? Pleasant requests, gentle reminders, and subtle interventions are needed here. Remarks such as "Honey, could you try to not be such a slob?" do not work (I say this from experience). If asking nicely and reminding gently do not work, perhaps a meeting is in order. If possible, provide a cup of tea and a slice of cake at the meeting. Making it a formal affair emphasizes the importance of your message and will make the new system seem more enjoyable to the trainee.

On Structured and Disciplined Living

Famille Chic led very disciplined lives with a lot of structure; they loved a routine and rarely strayed from it. So, for example, you would never see Monsieur Chic leave his pipe on the end table one night and on the kitchen table the next. He had a place for his pipe and it went in the same place every single night after he used it. No exceptions.

Maintaining a clutter-free home requires discipline. Start to observe your own habits as an outsider would. For example, when you come home, do you put your handbag in the same place every time? Or do you get distracted when walking through the front door so that your bag finds itself occasionally on the coffee table rather than in the hall closet? What about your dishes? After breakfast does the cereal bowl end up almost in the dishwasher but not quite?

You can train yourself by creating a routine. For example, if you never leave your bedroom slippers in the same place twice, pick a place for them and get into the habit of leaving them there every night. At the foot of the bed, for example. This discipline can be applied to almost everything that you have: shoes, coats, newspapers, magazines, etc.

Putting things in their proper place is really quite easy and takes much less time than the alternative—which is searching for them every time you need them. That cereal bowl sitting by the sink could have easily gone in the dishwasher and out of sight. Why deal with the cereal bowl twice?

This reminds me of the time my mother-in-law came to visit us from London. One afternoon she was kindly watching the baby for me while I had the luxury of taking a much needed shower and washing, then blow-drying my hair. As any woman who has had small children knows, that is a luxury, indeed! When I looked at the clock, I realized how much time I had taken and was worried that my mother-in-law might wish to go back to her hotel. So instead of putting away all my hair care paraphernalia (blow-dryer, wide-barrel brush, several clips, and two bottles of styling products), I got dressed and went upstairs to thank her for watching the baby. I figured I would clean the mess up later. It turned out she did not need to be back at her hotel, and we played with the baby a little while longer. At one point my mother-in-law had to go into our bathroom to get something. Because I was preoccupied with playing with the baby, I had forgotten about the complete state of disarray our master bathroom was in! I normally keep it very tidy and wouldn't think twice about her going in there. Later that day after she left, I returned to my bathroom and looked around in dismay at the messy clutter I had left for her to see.

It would have taken me only one minute to put all that clutter away, but I hadn't done it. Of course the one time I let it slip, my mother-in-law (who keeps immaculate homes) happens to see it! This offshoot of Murphy's Law is very similar to the one discussed earlier: if you leave the house looking like a frump, you will run into an ex-lover or frenemy. Let's just say that after the bathroom incident I learned my lesson! Now I try under all circumstances to keep my surroundings as tidy as possible. (With small children, sometimes that is not very tidy—but every little bit helps!)

Managing Everyday Items

It is important to have a hidden place to keep one's keys, cell phone, wallet, sunglasses, and purse. This place is preferably by the front door so that these items can be tucked away immediately. It is also handy always to have your keys in the same place so you never lose them.

I never saw Famille Chic's keys, wallets, or mobile phones hanging around the house and they would *never* be on the coffee table. Finding a place for one's keys and handbag doesn't sound like it should be such a problem—but alas, for me it was. It was a major issue in our home, and it frustrated me so! In our town home, we do not have a traditional entryway. The front door opens to stairs that lead up to our living room. So the entry to our home does not have an obvious place to house all these daily-use items. There was a closet at the top of the stairs, however, that I thought would be perfectly suitable. Yet every day when we came home, my husband and I would place our things on the dining room table, rather than in the hall closet. Why were we so opposed to placing our items in our hall closet— where I felt they belonged? I decided to investigate.

Our hall closet was horribly stuffed. There were so many coats and jackets hanging in there that if a guest came over, there wasn't room for another coat! So the guest's coat and handbag would inevitably go on the back of a dining room chair—not a good option. Especially if they have come to dine and you need to move the coat once everyone goes to the table. The whole situation bothered me. I would dream about having someone over, asking if I could take my guest's coat, and hanging it neatly in the hall closet. But in reality, if I opened the closet door, there was a very good chance that tennis rackets, umbrellas, and other miscellaneous objects would fly out—embarrassing us all.

The hall closet should only house the coats you wear most often and around four padded or wooden hangers for your guest's coats. Be aware of your shoe storage too. We were using our hall closet to store every shoe we've ever owned. There were so many shoes, they were piled on top of the vacuum cleaner (it is necessary for us to store our vacuum cleaner in the hall closet), so every week when the housekeeper pulled out the vacuum, she would scream (and probably silently curse me) when a pile of excess shoes jumped out at her.

I ended up pulling everything out of the closet, and as you

can probably guess, a lot of it was headed for the trash can or charity shop. I found old travel pillows, receipts, ten-year-old Ugg boots (!), and exercise equipment we'd never used!

After cleaning out the closet, I hung an over-the-door storage bag to house our miscellaneous items. It has taken some time to change our habits and actually use the closet, but now we do, and our dining room table is clear and ready for use at all times.

Once you become aware of the areas of clutter in your home, you develop a sensitivity toward them. Suddenly a cluttered drawer or a cluttered corner that didn't bother you before starts to bother you . . . big-time. With the aid of our housekeeper I had gotten rid of most of the junk drawers in our home. There were two drawers, however, that I never got around to doing—and it turned out they were the most important. My husband and I have a nightstand on either side of our bed in the master bedroom. In our nightstand drawers was everything from coins to pens to lighters to books to magazines and catalogs. What a mess! This clutter was right by our heads for eight hours a night while we slept. One night I couldn't sleep because I was thinking about the unorganized mess just inches away. I organized the drawers the very next day.

More tips on maintaining a clutter-free home

- Create a filing system to deal with the mail. Recycle the junk mail immediately and store the bills and important correspondence in a receptacle or file folder (again, hidden away) to deal with at a later date.

- Invest in furniture that doubles as storage. We purchased a large tufted ottoman to use as a coffee table. We love it because it opens like a trunk and stores all our remotes, game controls, and DVDs.

Living a clutter-free existence can be highly rewarding. You deserve to live well and in a beautiful space. Your possessions deserve to be housed with respect. When you live in a clutter-free environment, you set the standard of living a quality life at home. You will reap benefits in innumerable ways.

Le Recap

- Analyze which areas of your home require decluttering. Be honest with yourself.

- Tackle each clutter hot spot slowly and don't take on more than you can handle in any given decluttering session.

- Keep your closets, drawers, and cupboards clutter-free. Because we tend to hide clutter in these storage spaces, we don't have proper space for our everyday items.

- Cut down on how much you bring into the home. Only go shopping for things you really need.

- Figure out a system that works for the other people in your home. Make sure everyone is on board with your plan.

- Deal with things like filing and mail as soon as possible to avoid clutter catastrophes.

- Live a structured life at home and be strict with yourself about keeping everything in its place.

Chapter 13

SEEK OUT THE ARTS

Although you might not guess it based on the prior chapters, I didn't actually go to Paris to lounge, gallivant, and observe lifestyle traits, but rather went to study and further my education. I studied French, theatre, and art history, and the city was my classroom. On Monday, for example, we would discuss a painting in art history class, and on Wednesday we would go see it at one of the major Paris museums, perhaps the Musée d'Orsay or the Louvre. In theatre we would read a play—such as Molière's *Le bourgeois gentilhomme*—as an assignment, and then the following week we would go see the live production at La Comédie Française. As you can imagine, I was in heaven.

This total immersion in the arts was an exquisite experience for me. Not only were we shown the world-famous institutions such as the Louvre and the Paris Opera, but our professors introduced us to smaller, less well known museums and theatres.

One experience I'll never forget was seeing Ionesco's *La cantatrice chauve* (*The Bald Soprano*) at a tiny theatre that sat only fifty people. We were so close to the actors, it almost felt as if we were onstage ourselves!

I have always been interested in the arts, particularly theatre (I was a theatre major in college), but I had never incorporated them so wholly into my life as I did in Paris. As a result, my life felt richer and more fulfilling. Attending the theatre or an art exhibit every week kept me mentally fit. Rather than sitting around discussing the latest celebrity scandal, my friends and I were discussing things of merit. We would analyze plays and films. We had philosophical discussions. I gained a greater understanding of myself and I felt like a participant in the culture I enjoyed.

Music

When I was a child, I took piano lessons for several years. I also played saxophone in the school band. (My friends now are always amused to find I played the saxophone. I just tell them I wanted to be exactly like Lisa Simpson!) The high school wind ensemble would gather in the music hall before school started and rehearse for an hour and a half. I complained about getting up so early, but I had to admit, starting out the day by creating music was a wonderful treat.

I like to have music playing all throughout the day (as I write this I am listening to Yo-Yo Ma's *La Voix du Violoncelle*). Listening to music can really bring you out of any funk you might happen to be in. It can also inspire creativity. I never sit down to write without playing inspirational music first. It isn't always classical—although classical is my favorite. I listen to everything from Paul Simon to John Legend to Robin Thicke to Coldplay to Yo-Yo Ma. If you feel as though you've been going through life without passion or on autopilot, introduce music into your life. Maybe as a child you played a musical instrument. Or when you were in college, you had Dave Matthews Band or Bob Dylan always playing in your dorm room. Those were carefree, passionate days, weren't they? There's no reason our days now can't be the same.

The rapture that Famille Chic displayed when they listened to their classical music after dinner was refreshing. They were connoisseurs of music and made it an important part of daily life. You can do the same. How nice would it be to play music after dinner rather than having the whole family zonk out on the couch in front of the TV? Music can really create a special atmosphere in the home, and yet many people only play it when company is coming over. I like to play music at all hours of the day. It's not constantly on but can be turned on at any moment for an impromptu dance session (very handy for incorporating exercise into your day). Also, every morning when I give the children their breakfast, I like to have music playing. It's a nod to my high school wind ensemble days when I started the day off with music. It just gets everything going on the right foot.

If you would like to take it a step further, why not start a musical group of your own? Alexander McCall Smith, one of my favorite writers, is a member of the Really Terrible Orchestra, or RTO—a group of amateur British musicians who come together to create music. They are very upfront about the amateur nature of their abilities (hence the name), but they have lots of fun and now have fans all over the world.

When I lived in Paris, there was music all around me. Many times it came in the form of accordion players who hopped on the metro to collect tips. But one evening, I discovered a special treat. It was at one of Madame Bohemienne's wild dinner parties, where a few artistic types were the guests of honor, that I learned about the secret midnight quartet at the Louvre.

"You haven't heard about the Louvre at midnight?" they asked me astonished, as I had already been in Paris for a few months.

"Non!" I replied, leaning in over my coq au vin. "Do tell!"

Madame Bohemienne's guests told us that every so often (usually once a week—but one could never tell—and rarely on the same day) a group of musicians played a free concert in the courtyard of the Louvre at midnight. It was spectacular—so special, so romantic! We had to go.

And we did. I'm not sure how we found out which night the quartet was playing, but one crisp evening in early spring, my friends and I wandered into one of the courtyards of the Louvre and found a string quartet. Only a handful of people were scattered around the courtyard listening to the beautiful music. There were no chairs; people either sat on the edge of the fountain or on a blanket or scarf laid on the ground.

The quartet played beautifully for about an hour—Mozart, Chopin, Brahms. I remember sitting there feeling rapturous—grateful that I was there under the stars in that beautiful city, by that beautiful building that held some of the world's most important pieces of art, surrounded by friends and listening to this "secret concert"—and feeling that life was truly good, indeed . . .

I'm not sure if the secret concerts at the Louvre are still held at midnight, but if they are and you find yourself in Paris . . . *allez,* I tell you. *Allez . . .*

Visual Arts

Madame Bohemienne was a patron of the arts. She delighted constantly in the exhibitions at the Centre Pompidou and usually invited artistic types over for her wild dinner parties. One evening we accompanied her to the Centre Pompidou for a private showing of a collection of sketches and sculptures by Alberto Giacometti. That evening was magical. It seemed I saw art everywhere I went in Paris.

Do you remember Professeur Immaculate, my beauty-loving art history professor in Paris? His amazing class forever changed how I view art.

Some of my favorite moments in Paris were spent in museums with Professeur Immaculate. We stopped, we regarded, we took it all in. We all stood in shock in front of Gustave Courbet's *The Origin of the World*. We noted the moral message in Thomas Couture's debauched masterpiece, *Romans of the Decadence*. We regarded with amusement how the form of the woman changed in Picasso's paintings through the course of his marriage as he became increasingly bitter toward his wife. I particularly liked portraits. If the painter is good (and if featured in the Louvre or Musée d'Orsay, he or she inevitably is), a portrait can capture the soul of the subject. One of my favorite portraits was done by Edouard Manet of Berthe Morisot, the nineteenth-century painter. She is in black mourning attire, holding a small bouquet of violets—her expression mysterious and, at the same time, vulnerable.

I'm not going to lie: before living in Paris, I felt that museums were a tad boring. I would occasionally attend an exhibit at a museum or gallery in Los Angeles—but usually only if one of the big names came into town—van Gogh or Picasso, for example. But after studying with Professeur Immaculate, the world of art sprang to life for me. If you are able to take an art appreciation class in your community or at your local museum, do. Learning to appreciate art can change the way you see the world around you.

Discover your local museums. Many of us live in big cities and have only been to our major museums once or twice, writing them off as tourist destinations. Yet when we travel, we will inevitably visit museums in foreign cities. I'm very fortunate to live close to both of the Getty Museums, in Los Angeles and Malibu. Entry to those museums is free—what a gift to the community! I try to go as often as I can. In fact, my good friend Jen and I like to take our babies to museums or art exhibits to shake up the traditional playdate. After all, children are never too young to appreciate art.

If you don't live in a metropolitan area, you might have to work a little harder to seek out galleries or museums, but when you do, you might find some gems. If you are frustrated with the art available in your area, why not put on a showing of your own? Most of us know people with artistic inclinations—whether it's painting, sculpting, drawing, textiles, ceramics, etc. Collect works from a single artist or a group of artists, display them in your home, and throw a cocktail party to celebrate. Bring the art to you.

Theatre

Theatre is a subject very near to my heart. It was my major in college, and in my teens and early twenties I did a lot of theatre. Along with acting on the stage, I had (and still have) a passion for viewing live theatre. Whether it is a small production like *La cantatrice chauve* in a tiny, independent space or a grand operatic production at the Paris Opera, there is no doubt about it—a night at the theatre can be a magical experience.

We all watch way too much television and see too little theatre. Get season tickets to your local playhouse. You will no doubt meet interesting people in the audience. I have seen a lot of theatre in my lifetime, and my favorite experiences have been attending the small productions with unknown actors in community theatres. There is something about watching a live performance that is thrilling.

You could take it even a step further—if you've always wanted to act, why not audition for a play in your local community or church theatre? Or if you fancy yourself a director or stagehand or producer, why not go for it and try to put on your own production?

When in Paris, I saw Yasmina Reza's production of *Trois versions de la vie*. Yasmina Reza is a playwright and actress who oftentimes stars in her own productions. I was deeply impressed with this multifaceted woman. Take the cue from Yasmina Reza or from the Really Terrible Orchestra and stage your own production. It is never too late to do this, and you might just spark a wonderful artistic trend in your community. Take the plunge. I miss my theatre days very much and plan to return to the theatre at a later date. (Perhaps when I am not busy raising children and writing books!)

Films

My favorite film is *Amélie,* or as it is known in France, *Le fabuleux destin d'Amélie Poulain* (*The Fabulous Destiny of Amélie Poulain*). I have probably seen this film thirty times by now, but the first time I saw it was in Paris on a class trip. We watched the entire film, which is in French, without English subtitles. I was entranced by the innovative and revolutionary cinematography, by the hauntingly beautiful musical score, by the charismatic lead actress, Audrey Tautou, and by the passion behind the simple story of how Amélie loved to help change other people's destinies while sorely neglecting her own. This love story moved me so greatly, I cried watching it, and as soon as I got back to America, I went to see it in a movie theatre again (and eventually bought the DVD) so I could read the subtitles and not miss a thing. Jean-Pierre Jeunet, the director, recently came to Santa Monica and spoke at a screening of *Amélie* at the independent Aero Theatre. I couldn't find anyone to go with me, so I attended it by myself and enjoyed every second of the film just as though I were back in Paris again.

It is moments like these in the cinema that make film so powerful. I am a strong believer in seeking out independent films. I love to see foreign films because the stories are less commercial and can give fascinating glimpses into the lives of people in countries that we might never travel to. If you find that you crave independent films but can't find anyone to go with you, why not go by yourself? Now that I'm back in California, I tend to go alone more often than not. There is something very decadent about going to the cinema by yourself in the middle of the day—getting a popcorn and soda (or tea in my case—for some reason I like tea at the cinema) and watching a film, uninterrupted. Bliss!

Seek out the arts, wherever you live.

- If you live in a large city and have access to a lot of cultural activities, take full advantage—attend the symphony, the theatre, the ballet, the opera. Visit art galleries. Attend book readings and listen to writers' talks.
- Reacquaint yourself with a musical instrument. Many of us learned a musical instrument as children. For me it was the piano and saxophone. I recently took up the piano again and find joy in playing.
- Join a book club or your local writers' group.
- Write that novel you've always wanted to write. My writing teacher and mentor Alan Watt has recently published

his book *The 90-Day Novel.* It is the ultimate writer's tool to help you get the words on the page.

- Stage a poetry reading. You could have a theme, such as Romantic or Gothic poetry. Read the works of great poets aloud or read original pieces.
- Put on a play in your living room. It could be a one-act play or a series of short plays or even a night of improv. (This is especially fun if you are dealing with amateurs. That way the pressure is off and you know it is okay to laugh!)

Back in Los Angeles I keep on my toes by seeking out independent theatre and film, attending art galleries, and listening to live music. The benefits of being a patron of the arts is perhaps one of the most important lessons I learned while living in Paris because it is an aspect of my life that brings me so much joy—a joy that I look forward to passing on to my daughters.

Le Recap

- Totally immerse yourself in the arts and live a culturally fulfilling life.

- Play music throughout your day as a soundtrack to your life.

- Keep au courant with your local museum's latest art exhibits and attend them.

- Attend theatre regularly—whether you patronize large productions or local independent endeavors.

- Bring the arts into your home and get your friends involved.

- Become an artist yourself. Pick up an instrument, write that book you've always wanted to write, audition for your local play, or get out the paintbrushes. Relish the process and get creative!

Chapter 14

CULTIVATE AN AIR OF MYSTERY

My bedroom in Famille Chic's apartment looked out onto a courtyard. Because we were a few floors up, my window had a direct view of the window of our neighbor, whose apartment was across the courtyard. This neighbor was very mysterious. He seemed interested in me. Almost every morning when I pulled back the curtains in my room, he would be at his window looking out with a cup of coffee. (I guess he didn't drink his morning beverage out of a bowl!) In the beginning I was quite shy, so I would either draw the curtains back or scurry out of sight and just peek through a gap in the thick drapes to get a better glimpse of him. One time he caught me doing this and smiled at me and raised his coffee cup.

Thus began a five-month-long flirtation with my mysterious neighbor. At one point during every day we would see each other through the window. He would smile at me and wave and I would smile back. Sometimes we held each other's glance for a little longer than one would for an average hello. Occasionally he had a woman over and I would see her through the window. I was surprised to feel a twinge of jealousy. What was happening? I never met the mysterious neighbor in person—not even once. In a way, I'm glad I never did.

The thing that was so alluring about this man was that I knew nothing about him. He had an air of mystery. I let my imagination run away with me, of course. He was single and relatively young, living in the Sixteenth Arrondissement. I fancied he was a successful writer, maybe of crime fiction, or perhaps a sculptor. Or maybe he was a cinematographer! The mysterious smiles we exchanged were fueled by wonder. If I had met him by the mailboxes and found out more about him, he might not have been so alluring. What if I found out he had two ex-wives and a drinking problem? That would have been the end of the flirtation right there!

But, of course, even if he had two ex-wives and a propensity for the sauce, he never would have told me if we'd met, because in France people like to maintain an air of mystery.

French people, as a habit, do not reveal too much informa-

Lessons from Madame Chic

tion about themselves. Not to people they know and certainly not to strangers.

This is not the case in America. A few months after having my baby, I treated myself to my first manicure/pedicure in a long time. Being somewhat sleep-deprived and feeling highly unglamorous, I was really looking forward to the experience. I did have a wonderful time (mani-pedi and ten-minute shoulder massage . . . heaven!) but the experience was marred by the woman in the chair next to me, who was speaking loudly on her cell phone during my entire treatment. She shared lurid details about her date the night before, her status on match.com, the woeful details of her dwindling bank account, and the fact that she hates her boss. Not only did she share these things with her friend on the phone, she shared them with me and an entire salon full of women.

That would never happen in France.

Living in Paris, I never heard French people speaking loudly on a cell phone in public about their private lives. They might have a few confidants to whom they tell their innermost secrets, but I can assure you that this sharing is not done on their cell phone in the nail salon. (In fact, it would be much more French to enjoy your manicure, pedicure, and massage thoroughly, without spoiling the peaceful experience by stressing out on your cell phone!)

I was quick to judge the lady in the nail salon, but when I turned a critical eye on myself, I realized that maintaining an air of mystery is actually quite difficult! I noticed my propensity to overshare details of my life, my intolerance of silence in a conversation, and my need to please people.

Wise Man Seldom Talks

I was dining in a Chinese restaurant recently where my fortune cookie read, "Wise man seldom talks." It's true, and speaking only when necessary can do wonders for your air of mystery. When you guard what comes out of your mouth and only share what you want to, when you want to, you gain power and presence.

For example, when you meet someone for the first time, what things do you talk about? Do you reveal more than you'd like to in an attempt to appear friendly?

If you are with a group of people and do not share many details of your life, others might accuse you of being cold or aloof. Stand your ground. Don't worry what others think of you. Chances are your air of mystery intrigues them and they are merely jealous.

Become Comfortable with Silence

Are you okay with silence? Or do you try and fill it by talking or asking questions? I know that I have a *major* problem with silence. When speaking with someone, whether I know them or not, I will babble or giggle nervously at the first sign of silence in a desperate attempt to avoid awkwardness. Talk about the opposite of an air of mystery!

I have slowly come to understand there is nothing wrong with silence. In fact it can be quite delicious. It only has to be awkward if you make it so. Practicing being okay with silence is something I have to do on a daily basis.

A neighbor of mine is quite mysterious; he travels a lot and is often out of town. (What is it with me and mysterious neighbors?) He has his air of mystery mastered: whenever I see him, he alludes to his travels but does not tell me what he does for a living (and, like the French, I would *never* ask). Our conversations are usually peppered with pauses. He is very comfortable with silence. I am not. Inevitably at the first sign of silence I say something lame and unmysterious and laugh shrilly. Not because I am interested in him particularly, but because this is what I do with *everybody*. It is a malady of mine.

So one day I decided to practice cultivating my air of mystery with my mysterious neighbor. I saw him while I was taking Gatsby out for his morning walk. I had the baby on my chest in the BabyBjörn and Gatsby on his leash. It had been a particularly long night of not sleeping (the baby was teething), so I employed one of my techniques for looking presentable always by wearing a long coat over my pajamas. I must have looked silly because it was about 80 degrees outside and there I was in a winter coat complete with baby and dog—but never mind. At least I wasn't showing off my pajamas.

This is how our conversation went:
"Hello," said the mysterious neighbor.
"Hello," said I.
[Long pause!]

MN: How are you?

J: I'm great, thank you. How are you?

MN: Life is treating me well. [Another long pause!] And you, are you happy?

J: Yes, very. [This time I paused!] I haven't seen you recently, you must have been traveling.

MN: I have. Doing a lot of traveling and a lot of work.

J: How wonderful. [Another pause—Yes! I can do this!] It was lovely to see you.

MN: And you.

J: Good-bye.

I'm not going to lie, the long pauses were excruciating for me. But I stuck with it and was rather pleased with the result. Nothing of substance was said, but in these particular circumstances, things of substance aren't generally said anyway. I have a close circle of friends who know my life story and day-to-day activities, but for everyone else, I would like to remain mysterious.

That's why this exercise was very important for me. Normally at the first sign of silence I would have laughed uncomfortably and said something to my neighbor about the weather or apologized for my appearance or made a joke about how the baby is teething and I am a zombie on three hours of sleep. But I remained mysterious. Hey, it's a start!

What *Is* There to Talk About?

You may wonder what there is to talk about when you maintain an air of mystery. The answer is *everything!* Everything except for your life story, that is. After attending my fair share of dinner parties both chez Famille Chic and chez Famille Bohemienne, I came to wonder why I found their dinner guests to be so fascinating. I would have entire conversations with people about recent films, the latest art exhibit at the Centre Pompidou, or philosophical quandaries and walk away from the conversation not knowing where my new friends were from or what they did for a living. Sometimes I didn't even know their names!

I'm not suggesting that at your next dinner or cocktail party you should sulk in the corner with a pout on your face. Not at all! Be active, be vibrant, and join in the conversation. Talk about art, a great book you just read, current events, an interesting film you recently saw. Be alive, be interesting, and contribute to the conversation. Conversations can be so formulaic these days (What did you do for the holidays? What are your plans for the weekend?) Get your kicks out of an unpredictable and real conversation—see where it takes you! You will become intriguing to the other guests. You will be known as someone with a lot to say—and not in a bad way. We've all been to parties where people go on and on about their life—their problems, their dramas. It can be such a bore. Those people are not mysterious! Don't fall into that trap. Let people wonder about you.

Practice makes perfect. "Have you read any good books lately?" is an excellent question to ask someone you just met. The answer will reveal a great deal about your new acquaintance. If she hesitates for a long time, she probably doesn't read very much (in which case you should probably change the subject), or she might have some great book recommendations for you. What a fun way to reveal one's hand.

In France it is considered rude to ask people what they do for a living. Never ask this question. You might never find out or they might tell you. But then again, do you really want to know? Remember my mysterious French neighbor? Not knowing what he did for a living really fascinated me.

It is also important to refrain from gossiping about other people—not only to preserve your air of mystery but also because gossiping is just bad energy. This can be hard when the entire table is participating. Let's say the conversation veers to something that makes you uncomfortable—gossip about a mutual acquaintance, for example. You have two choices—you can stay or you can leave the conversation. If you are seated at a dinner table, it may be quite hard to leave. In that case, just don't participate in the conversation. If you are asked your opinion on the subject, say something flippant like, "I don't wish to comment on that." Say it with a twinkle in your eye—no need to get too serious. Your dinner guests will be intrigued as to why you are not participating in the gossip session, and you will look better for it.

To Whom Can You Talk about Yourself?

You may be wondering when it *is* appropriate to discuss the intimate details of your life. After all, it can feel really good to unload a problem or commiserate every now and then with other people. I recommend having one or two people in your life whom you trust and who are very close to you. A sister, a cousin, a best friend. We all have someone like this. Share your intimate details about life with this person or persons. It is a comfort to talk about what's on your mind.

Let's say you had a fight with your husband. He keeps putting his dirty laundry at the base of the laundry bin rather than *inside* the laundry bin. He's been doing this for three years. You can't take it anymore—what's his problem? You exploded and yelled at him. You are not proud of yourself, but there it is. He got defensive and stormed out of the house. You are upset. You call your best friend. Hopefully she will put it into perspective for you by telling you there are worse things that could happen.

You laugh about it. You make up with your husband when he gets home. You have all moved on (you know your friend will not bring it up again; you have an understanding). But if you are in the habit of telling all your acquaintances about your drama, you end up repeating the story several times and give it more power. It was a petty fight, but by your repeating the story, it becomes something much more. Petty fights are highly unmysterious.

Just be sure that you don't use this one person as a repository for *all* your problems. Be respectful of her time and pick and choose what you tell her. If you find you are becoming a bit of a drama queen, it might be time to adopt an air of mystery with your best friend too! Ask her about her life for a change.

Never Downplay Your Success

Do you receive compliments graciously? Mysterious people always do. If I were to compliment Madame Chic on her blouse, she would never say, "What? This old thing? I got it on clearance!" She would say, *"Merci,"* and that would be it.

When someone compliments you, just say thank you. Take the compliment and smile. Maybe return a compliment (if you sincerely mean it).

Also never downplay your success to make other people feel better. If things are going great in your life but you know someone who is not in such a fortunate position, it can be tempting to downplay your happiness in order to make her feel better. You might bring up a fight you and your girlfriend had a month ago in order to contribute to the "woe is me" tone of the conversation. Avoid this. There is no need to rehash negativity. If your friend is experiencing a hard time, you simply need to offer her support. What is so alluring about mysterious people is that they seem deliciously contented. You want to know their secrets! So if you are contented, be contented and don't apologize for it.

Romantic Relationships

Maintain an air of mystery in your amorous relationships. Chances are you did this in the beginning of your courtship. You would never have, for example, clipped your toenails in front of your love on your first date. Those things would be done behind closed doors, preferably before he even came over. So why is it okay to do it four years later when you are married and have two kids?

When you have the urge to tell your partner something very mundane (like how the grapes gave you gas), pause and perhaps say nothing at all. If you were about to say something but caught yourself and he asks what you were going to say, just smile and say, "Oh, nothing." He will be intrigued.

When grooming and taking care of personal matters, always do it behind closed doors. Your lover does not need to be privy to your daily use of the neti pot, nor does he need to see you plucking your eyebrows. I know couples who brag about how they pee in front of each other (I shudder to even type this).

That is not intimacy, that is just gross. Maintain an air of mystery with your lover and keep the romance alive.

Be Yourself

Cultivating an air of mystery is not to be confused with being fake, putting on airs, or trying to be someone you are not. It is simply being yourself without hiding behind a wall of people pleasing. It's about not exchanging fake pleasantries or sharing truths about yourself with people who are not terribly important to you. So be in the moment, and be yourself fully. Value the air of mystery that draws people to you.

Further techniques

- Acquire a Mona Lisa smile. This is a tad clichéd, but it is a strategy worth mentioning. A subtle half smile suggests that you know something. And inevitably the other person will want to know what that is. Never, of course, tell them. They will go mad.
- Speak softly. Use your inside voice. When you speak softly, people will feel compelled to lean in to hear what you have to say. Very mysterious.
- Be a good listener.

Le Recap

- Guard your words and never overshare. Speak when necessary.

- Become comfortable with silence.

- Avoid telling people your life story when you first meet them. Instead, talk about things like art, philosophy, or current events. Make yourself interesting so they wonder about you.

- Have one or two trusted friends to share your intimate secrets with.

- Learn to receive compliments graciously.

- Remember (not just in France, but wherever you are), never ask someone what they do for a living.

- Keep the romance alive in your relationship by not discussing every mundane detail of your daily life. Do all grooming behind closed doors. Your lover does not need to know *how* you look so good. He just needs to know that you do.

Chapter 15

PRACTICE THE ART OF ENTERTAINING

There are few things better, in my opinion, than attending a proper dinner party—with apéritifs, hors d'oeuvres, music, a properly set table, interesting guests, excellent cuisine, dessert, cheese course, coffee, and digestif. The experience can be divine. *Throwing* a dinner party, on the other hand, can be very daunting.

France is truly a dinner party culture, and in Paris, entertaining is a part of life. Madame Chic and Madame Bohemienne entertained guests *at least* once a week. And I'm not talking about having the neighbor over for a cup of tea. They both threw elaborate dinner parties frequently. In fact, I attended more dinner parties in Paris than I have in my entire life before or since.

Madame Chic and Madame Bohemienne had very different styles when it came to their dinner parties. Madame Chic's were always elegant affairs—classical music, apéritifs in the salon beforehand, delicious five-course meal to follow, then some after-dinner smoking for the men, digestifs, and more classical music. Her guests were usually conservative, well-respected upper-crust types.

Madame Bohemienne, on the other hand, had more wild, passionate parties. Her guests were often from the art world. Whereas Madame Chic's apéritifs consisted of whiskey or port, Madame Bohemienne loved champagne cocktails. Her dinners were not elegant five-course meals but usually consisted of three more casual courses, and afterward . . . well, I never could really remember what happened afterward, we were having that much fun.

I liked each style for different reasons and always marveled at how these women would pull off these successes frequently and without a bit of stress. For them, entertaining was an art.

The Confident Hostess

The key to the success of Madame Chic and Madame Bohemienne's dinner parties was confidence, *major* confidence. Those women were master planners; their signature was in every last detail. Everything from the music to the food to the guests to the ambience was by their design. They genuinely seemed to enjoy every moment. Entertaining was just another part of life. There were no harried freak-out sessions in the kitchen or stressed-out scenes about the food. If something went wrong, you would never have known it—their attitudes as hostesses were practically Zen-like.

Of course, having confidence as a hostess is much easier said than done. I should know. In the past I was not the most masterful of hostesses. I recall a rather painful dinner party where I made a chicken curry as the only dish served other than rice. The curry had carrots in it, and I found out with dismay that our female guest was severely allergic to carrots. *Quel désastre!* My guest was gracious and ate around them, but I was traumatized by the incident and didn't entertain again for a whole year.

Madame Chic was a no-nonsense woman. She seemed to be confident in everything she did—cooking, entertaining, communicating. A carrot allergy wouldn't have phased her. Her confidence made me feel at ease. Have you ever been to a dinner party where the host or hostess was harried—even exasperated? Nothing makes a guest feel more uncomfortable than a hostess who keeps apologizing. No matter what happens, just own it and never apologize for your hostessing skills.

If you would like to be a confident hostess, here are some

important concepts to remember. Channel your inner Madame Chic and tell yourself the following:

Your guests (presumably) like you very much and want you to succeed. Honestly, most people are just thrilled to get an invitation to something. So you do not need to worry about their judging you and your hosting skills. In California I rarely get invited to people's homes for dinner parties. I'm being optimistic by assuming this isn't because I haven't any friends but because people don't entertain at home anymore. They are either too tired, too busy, or too afraid. What a bore! I miss the active social calendar I had in Paris. I would be delighted to go to a dinner party, tea party, housewarming party—anything, really! (Yes, friends, I am open for invitations.) If you invite guests into your home, they will be thrilled to be there. I know I would. They will not notice all the little things that have not gone as planned. If they are true friends, they will just be happy to be in your company and will want your party to be a success. If they don't, then they shouldn't be in your home in the first place.

You look fabulous (providing you put some effort into your appearance). If you put any effort into your appearance by dressing nicely and grooming yourself (clean hair and any variation of *le no-makeup look* are perfectly acceptable), you have nothing to worry about. Smile, let your hair down (but remember your good posture), and just flow through the evening. Don't worry about that tiny spot of grease on your dress or wonder how your hair is holding up. Let go and be in the moment. *Know* that you look beautiful.

The food tastes great, and if it doesn't, it's not the end of the world. I have a disclosure to make. Madame Bohemienne was not the best cook—certainly not as skilled as Madame Chic. The meat was often overdone and the stews were . . . well, stewy. But we never minded. Her confidence as a hostess made up for the cooking and we always had a great time. In fact, her dinner parties were so much fun, I felt flutters of excitement when I would be invited to her home.

Go with what you know. If you do not feel comfortable or ready to throw a five-course dinner party like Madame Chic, start small and perhaps in a different genre. I love to throw tea parties—they are just easier to pull off. The more I throw them, the more comfortable I get and the more elegant the affairs become. I started off by serving fruit and a homemade cake along with coffee or tea, and I have now graduated to more intricate affairs. As I write this, it is the eve of the royal wedding of William and Catherine and I am throwing a tea party tomorrow to celebrate. There will be five different types of sandwiches, two cakes, various other yummy nibbles, Pimm's cocktails, and (of course) tea. I am having the food catered because I do not have the time to make it myself. There is no shame in not making your own food—especially if you are not a great cook! Just make sure the food that you do offer is generous and enticing.

Calm down, let go, and most important . . . have fun! Entertaining isn't about being Martha Stewart perfect—it's about enjoying the company of your guests and making them feel welcome. Even though their dinner parties were so different, both Madame Chic and Madame Bohemienne were passionate about the food they cooked, the wine they served, and their guests. This enabled each of them to be in the moment, gliding effortlessly in the flow of the evening. Each was a gracious hostess who made you feel you were taking part in something special by being in her home. So no matter what happens, be positive, be optimistic, and smile (even if the dog jumps on the table and eats the mashed potatoes).

The Apéritif as Icebreaker

Famille Chic would always gather in the living room before dinner for some apéritifs and nibbles. An apéritif is a before-dinner drink that is said to stimulate the appetite. Apéritifs chez Famille Chic usually consisted of whiskey, port, or tomato juice. The port or tomato juices were served in charming little glasses, the whiskey in tumblers. Famille Chic never skipped this ritual.

The ritual of the apéritif was one of my favorite aspects about the French dinner party. It whetted my appetite and calmed my nerves. I was always nervous before any dinner party of Famille Chic's, especially in the beginning of my stay, because I was worried about speaking French. Would my grammar be acceptable? Would I understand everything that was said? Would I commit a faux pas? Trust me, after a glass of whiskey I wasn't thinking about *any* of those things. It loosened me up and I enjoyed the evening. Port was my favorite apéritif. Whiskey made things very fun. I had never actually had whiskey before living in Paris. Madame Chic's son gave me my first glass. He found it very amusing when I sputtered a bit after my first sip. My goodness, that stuff is strong! Every now and then I would take a tomato juice with Madame Chic so she didn't think I was a lush. I actually haven't had whiskey since my stay in Paris. Somehow its allure does not translate in other settings. Its memory will remain comfortably in Madame Chic's ornate living room.

Madame Bohemienne observed the ritual of the apéritif as well. As you can probably guess, Madame Bohemienne's apéritifs were an entirely different affair. We would gather in her home and sit on a sofa that was artfully draped with colorful throws and pillows. There would be a bowl of nibbles (chips or pretzels) placed on the low coffee table. Madame Bohemienne would then bring out a large bowl and prepare her famous champagne cocktail before all her guests. If we didn't have her champagne cocktail, we had a *rhum de Martinique* cocktail. Both were delicious. She would always have jazz playing in the background, and we would get carried away with the nibbles, the cocktails, the music, and the conversation. Her guests were always interesting and ranged from hairdressers to artists to teachers.

Sometimes Madame Bohemienne got too carried away and we would sit with the apéritifs for an hour and a half or more before dinner was served. Sometimes we wouldn't go to the table until ten p.m.! As a Californian who is accustomed to eating quite early (I hear it's best for the metabolism), I would find myself practically starving and slightly tipsy when we would finally be called to the dinner table. Nobody else seemed to notice the late hour, so I told myself . . . *when in Rome!*

Madame Bohemienne's Champagne Cocktail

1 bottle of champagne or sparkling wine
2 (or more) jigs of Grand Marnier
½ cup simple syrup (equal parts water and
sugar boiled, then cooled)
3 or 4 limes, sliced or cut in wedges
1 large punch bowl

Pour the bottle of sparkling wine or champagne into the bowl, add the Grand Marnier and simple syrup, then crush and squeeze the limes, leaving the rind in for effect. This cocktail is a sparkling, effervescent joy and one that sets the mood for the festive evening ahead.

Madame Bohemienne's Rum Cocktail

rum from Martinique
sugar cane syrup
a splash of lemon

Combine any amount of the above ingredients to your taste depending on how strong, how sweet, or how sour you prefer your cocktail.

On Committing Faux Pas

At the first dinner party I ever attended chez Madame Bohemienne, I said something rather shocking. She had served yogurt for dessert (a common custom in France), and I remarked (in French) that French yogurt was much nicer than American yogurt because there were fewer preservatives in it. I didn't know the French word for preservatives, so I just said *preservatifs,* which unfortunately translates as "condoms." After I made the statement that there were "fewer condoms in French yogurt," I wondered why all the French people at the table either had perplexed looks on their faces or were blatantly laughing out loud.

In these circumstances it is best to have a sense of humor and move on. Obviously I was mortified, but I just raised my glass, said *"Santé!"* and laughed with the rest of them. It worked and I got out of my gaffe, but please learn from my mistake and avoid saying the word *preservatif* at any and all French dinner tables.

Create Your Own Memorable Evening

Madame Chic and Madame Bohemienne's dinner parties were memorable for different reasons. I always left Madame Chic's dinner parties (and when I say *left,* I mean I would retire to my bedroom) feeling as though I had attended a very classy, highbrow affair. I would leave Madame Bohemienne's feeling as though I'd spent a joyous and artistic evening. Decide what you will become known for with your parties. Create a ritual—one that people will associate with you and will come to love and look forward to at your gatherings.

Music

Music is key to creating a signature atmosphere. Madame Bohemienne's jazz always set the scene, as did Madame Chic's classical music. I prefer lively music for my dinner parties and gatherings. Some lovely compilations are available on iTunes;

one in particular called *French Dinner Party* is great for evening. Also Sidney Bechet's *Petite Fleur* is an excellent jazz album for lively dinner or cocktail parties.

It is important to match the music to the type of meal you plan on serving. One afternoon my husband and I had an English friend over for a Sunday roast. We went all out—roast beef, English peas, roast potatoes, Yorkshire pudding. The music I chose to play was a salsa album. I figured it was a hot afternoon in California and it had a lively, upbeat flair. At one point our guest remarked how delicious the food was but that he felt like he was having "an English roast in Honduras." Not quite the vibe I was going for. I now try to match the music to the theme of the meal.

For larger parties, if you really want to go over the top, enlist a musical friend or friends and throw an impromptu concert in your home after dinner is served. How fun would it be to gather everyone with their coffee or digestifs by the piano and sing a few songs? Maybe you have a friend who plays the violin or have a friend who sings. It can be very charming and unexpected to surprise your guests in this way. Just make sure that the concert is short and sweet (unless you are confident that everyone is loving it).

Poems

In Alexander McCall Smith's 44 Scotland Street series, each book ends with a dinner party, and each dinner party ends with a poem recited by the character Angus Lordie. I love this idea.

You could ask your guests to bring their favorite poems and have each person read after the dinner or during dessert. People might feel silly initially, but this could be quite fun. You could create a tradition and become known for your "poetic dinners."

The Oyster Party

One day I received a call from my boyfriend saying that Madame Bohemienne had a surprise for us and would I be able to come over for dinner that evening? I was intrigued and could hardly refuse. I took the forty-minute metro ride from the Sixteenth Arrondissement to chez Bohemienne and walked up those long flights of steps wondering what surprise could possibly await me.

It turned out Madame Bohemienne had just visited Brittany and had brought back with her an entire crate of fresh oysters. I nearly fainted with delight. Now, many people don't like oysters. I am not one of those people. I love oysters. *Mon Dieu,* how I love oysters! And I had never seen so many oysters. I eagerly helped set the table. We shucked oysters, put music on, opened a bottle of champagne, and sat down to feast.

Delicious is an inadequate word to describe that meal. The raw oysters (accompanied with mignonette sauce and big pieces of crusty French bread and creamy butter) were divine. The champagne bubbles delighted my tongue and left me feeling delirious. We ended with a delicious piece of Camembert and a slice of Madame Bohemienne's famous flourless chocolate cake.

It was a simple meal but one of the best I've ever had. I don't know how many oysters I ate that evening, but I felt like a heroine in Molière's *Le bourgeois gentilhomme*. It was wonderful to spoil ourselves in such a decadent manner!

The Cheese Party

One evening Madame Bohemienne invited us to attend a cheese party her neighbor in the Eleventh Arrondissement was throwing. We went, not knowing what to expect from a cheese party. Would there be a cheese board with cheddar and crackers? Perhaps some wine? We headed to the neighbor's flat, which was a charming, one-bedroom bohemian abode (like attracts like, you see) on the top floor of the building. The apartment was small but very welcoming. Other than our hostess, ourselves, and Madame Bohemienne, there were only a few other guests. As we gathered in the tiny apartment, lively music was playing and the energy was palpable.

The dinner began with a salad with chicken livers. I felt a bit squeamish about the livers. I'd never had them before but did not want to offend the hostess, so I partook (not bad, but I was still squeamish). Then the cheese tray came out. There were twelve different kinds of cheese—mainly ones I'd never heard of. They were delicious, ripe, stinky, and pungent. We dined on the cheese with slices of baguette, and for dessert there was a cake. And of course, wine was served throughout the evening.

The concept of the cheese party was charming, but it was not the most intriguing aspect of the evening. Our hostess, who was as warm and welcoming as any Parisian host I have encountered, seemed to have a health problem that caused her to regularly release gas. Either it was a health problem and she couldn't control it, or else she knew that she was passing gas (loud gas!) and didn't care. Perhaps she was senile and didn't know. Yes, our hostess kept farting right through the evening—*loudly*. And no one seemed to notice or care that it was happening! It was the proverbial elephant in the room. The hostess's daughter didn't show any signs of caring. She certainly didn't pull us aside and warn us—which I might have expected.

Of course the immature child in me wanted to laugh. I will admit it. Not at her, but at the sheer absurdity of the concept of a farting hostess. My boyfriend and I exchanged sidelong glances but otherwise could not look at each other in case we burst into laughter. Our hostess was oblivious to our amusement. She was animated, lively, and very passionate about the cheeses she was introducing to the young Americans.

That night in bed I thought about the hostess. So many of us attend social gatherings and are self-conscious the whole time. *Do I have spinach in my teeth? Did I look good in the picture that was just taken? Have I said the right thing?* But our hostess that evening went through the entire dinner party with chronic flatulence and still won us over by being warm, charming, and adept. "Cutting the cheese" (no pun intended) in public is a major faux pas, but she didn't seem self-conscious about it at all! If she could do that and still succeed, then certainly I could entertain. I honestly think passing gas at the dinner table could be the worst thing that could happen to me as a hostess. But our hostess that evening did it the whole night and we still loved her! If she could be such an endearing hostess, even with her impediment, why couldn't I?

A Final Word

Give yourself the joy of opening your home, gathering your friends, and creating traditions while sitting around the dinner table. Release your inhibitions with regard to being the perfect hostess and jump right in. The only way to get better is to practice.

Le Recap

- No matter what sort of entertaining you are doing, be a confident hostess. This is what your guests want. Even if you don't feel confident, fake it until it comes naturally to you.

- Put an effort into your appearance.

- Go with what you know. A simple meal that tastes good is much better than an elaborate meal with hits and misses (and is much less work).

- Remain calm in the event of a catastrophe and always maintain a sense of humor.

- Resurrect the ritual of the apéritif and adopt your own signature drink (alcoholic or non).

- If you commit a faux pas, simply laugh it off. We've all done it.

- Create a memorable evening by choosing the right music.

- And I'm sure you already know what this last one is going to be . . . Have fun with it! What is the point of going to all that trouble if you yourself are not going to have a good time?

Chapter 16

REJECT THE NEW MATERIALISM

When the guidance counselor in Paris first told me about the family I would be living with, I was pleasantly surprised. Famille Chic was a well-respected aristocratic family with an apartment in the desirable Sixteenth Arrondissement and a country house in Brittany. I would be living with Monsieur Chic, Madame Chic, and their twenty-three-year-old son. Apparently Madame Chic liked to take in foreign exchange students because all but one of her children were grown and living elsewhere and she welcomed the company. Famille Chic also liked to learn about other cultures. The counselor confided that I was assigned to one of the wealthier families in the program.

I was intrigued. Famille Chic sounded like a good match for me. I did enjoy the finer things in life . . . This was going to be a match made in heaven! In the taxi ride on the way to my new home, I imagined what their swanky Sixteenth Arrondissement apartment would look like. I envisioned plush sofas, flat-screen TVs, my own en suite bathroom (done up in marble, of course), a state-of-the-art kitchen . . . As you can see, I let my imagination run away with me.

As you already know, Famille Chic's apartment was quite different from what I had imagined. It was magnificent, but not in the sort of nouveau riche way I envisioned.

At first I thought Famille Chic might have been living in reduced circumstances, but then I considered their esteemed address, the beautiful (and probably priceless) antiques that adorned their interiors, and the general desirability of their large, luxurious flat, and I came to the conclusion that that was just the way they had always lived. That in France there is not an obsession with what is called "the new materialism." They are not a society that constantly consumes—going on shopping binges looking for the next gadget, the next upgrade, the latest *thing* (which, as we have discussed, accounts for why their homes are so enviably clutter-free).

Famille Chic had absolutely no interest in keeping up with the Joneses. For example, they had one car for the three of them (and it was a very modest and nondescript car—not flashy at all). They spent their money on the things that were important to them—high-quality food, excellent wine, and well-made clothing.

I found Famille Chic's utter rejection of the new materialism refreshing and their restraint as consumers admirable. To live well—to live within your means and to avoid the seduction of the material world. That is what I call prospering.

No matter how much money you have, it can be good to rein in your spending. It helps the environment to not consume so many products—think about how much waste could be saved! It cuts down on clutter, and you will not have to find new places to store all your stuff. It is good for your bank account; think about all the wonderful things you could do with the money you save. Psychologically, when you are not focused on finding your next purchase, you can think about many more meaningful things.

Everyday Purchases

It is fun to examine how Famille Chic still lived a luxurious and quality lifestyle without all the expected large purchases—

the flashy car, the high-tech kitchen, the souped-up entertainment system—but it is also intriguing to examine the nature of their everyday purchases. When Madame Chic went to the local *tabac,* she did not go with the intention of buying one thing and leave carrying ten.

Most of us have done this before. I've gone out to the drugstore because I was out of shampoo, but somehow when I got home, not only was there shampoo in my shopping bag, there was also gum, hair ties, a new nail polish, a chocolate bar, *Us Weekly,* Tylenol PM, bedroom slippers, leave-in conditioner, three different kinds of Chapstick, and a sunhat. I had planned to spend $6.99 but instead spent $69.99. How did this happen? It's as if a shopping demon had possessed me and relieved me of my good sense.

The next time you go into a store to make a purchase, be aware of what you need and what you don't. I like to write lists before I go shopping. This certainly helps in the grocery store. It allows me to focus and not overspend. Lists are not only for the grocery store, however. I like to write lists before I go about my day if there are errands that need to be run. A sample list might look like this:

Pick up dry cleaning.

Buy shampoo (and only shampoo!).

Buy lettuce, apples, and milk.

Buy ½ lb. specialty coffee.

Using a list keeps me on track. Even with a list, not over-spending in a day requires extreme discipline for those of us not used to putting limits on our purchases. Try to pay for things with cash. Using a debit or credit card for everyday purchases can be quite dangerous. When you carry and pay for things with cash, you become much more aware of how much money you are spending (and often wasting).

It can also be helpful to write down every purchase you make for an entire week. And I mean *every* purchase: your daily latte, the book of stamps, lunches out, nail polish remover, cloth-ing purchases—*everything*. Chances are, if you are like me, you will be shocked to see how much you spend on the small things throughout the week. Even if some of those purchases are one-offs, you still get a sense of how much money you've wasted and how much *stuff* you've consumed. I used to buy my drinks every day at coffee chains. I wouldn't just get a drip coffee. I would get a designer drink. After I did the experiment of writing down what I spent, I was amazed to see how much money I wasted. Now I mainly drink my drinks at home or take them to go in a thermos.

Just think how much money you could save each year if you got strict with yourself and did not spend freely on "everyday" items! That money could go into your retirement fund or go toward a great vacation. As an added bonus, your home would not be cluttered with the remnants of these everyday purchases.

Clothing

If you are in the habit of employing a ten-item wardrobe, you are already experiencing the freedom that comes with not being a slave to fashion. If you are still a slave to fashion, perhaps you should go back and reread the chapter "Liberate Yourself with the Ten-Item Wardrobe."

Having said that, shopping for clothes can be my Achilles' heel. I can spend less time debating the purchase of a two-hundred-dollar dress than I do worrying about spending three dollars for a basket of organic strawberries. This neurosis has decreased significantly now that I have whittled my closet down to a capsule wardrobe, but it still rears its illogical head every now and then.

One way to fight this battle is to not even go into the shops unless you specifically need something. One day, I was walking to the farmer's market where I like to pick up fresh, organic produce for the week. The farmer's market in Santa Monica is situated on the Third Street Promenade, which also happens to be a major shopping district. As I walked with the intent of purchasing only food, I passed by the window of one of my favorite shops. There was an attractive blouse in the window. I hesitated for a moment. I looked at the blouse in the window, I looked at my daughter (who was saying with her eyes, "Don't do it, Mommy!" or was that just my imagination?), I looked at the farmer's market a few feet away that wasn't going anywhere, and I thought I'd just pop into the store for a peek.

Of course it's never just a peek, and I somehow ended up in the dressing room trying on six items of clothing! I ended up purchasing the top. It was a white blouse that I thought would fit nicely into my summer wardrobe. I knew it was a basic top that I would get a lot of use out of, but even so I left slightly irritated with myself for getting it in the first place. Did it fit into my wardrobe nicely? Yes. But was it necessary to get? No. That day, I spent a lot more money than I needed to.

So the moral of this story is that unless you are looking for something specific to add to your capsule wardrobe, don't even go into the shops. Don't tempt yourself.

Pride—a Cautionary Tale

One afternoon my husband, Ben, and I drove to Beverly Hills to go shopping and have some lunch. The shopping trip was for Ben, who tends to go shopping only once or twice a year (he is a natural subscriber to the tenet of quality over quantity). He wanted a casual pair of trousers that were not jeans. He was thinking he wanted cargo pants but upscale ones. So we set out. We had only just alighted from our car when we walked past the boutique Brunello Cucinelli on Brighton Way. Lo and behold, the mannequin in the window was wearing a pair of light cotton cargo pants in navy blue—not too bulky and with a tapered leg. I stopped my husband and pointed to the pants. They were just what he was looking for. We went in.

Now, if you haven't been inside a Brunello Cucinelli boutique (which we hadn't at the time), I must say that it is lovely. Not only are the clothes beautifully made, designed, and displayed, but the staff is adept and courteous (which is actually hard to find these days!). Ben said he'd like to try the blue trousers that were featured in the window, and the helpful store clerk, a young man in his early twenties, placed a pair in the dressing room for him to try on. While he was trying on the trousers, I walked around and admired the women's clothing. I noticed there were no price tags on anything (which should have been the first red flag), but I didn't think any more about it and waited for my husband to step out of the dressing room. While I was waiting, the salesclerk poured me a glass of mineral water. What service! Oh, how I loved shopping in Beverly Hills!

Ben stepped out of the dressing room and I exclaimed with delight that the trousers fit him perfectly. He is quite tall and has a hard time finding clothes that fit his frame. He said he loved them too. We both agreed that he should definitely get them. The salesclerk beamed. Ben then asked if they came in any other colors. They did. Before he said he would take the other color too (as I knew he was just about to do), I had the bright idea to ask how much the trousers were. Now, I knew they were going to be expensive, as we were in a very high-end shop. But they were just cargo pants, after all; how much could they possibly be? The salesclerk said, "The pants are six hundred ten dollars."

There was a long moment of silence. You could probably have knocked my husband over with a feather. I made a joke about how we wouldn't be needing the other color (you know my propensity to joke during awkward silences). Stunned, and as though in slow motion, we both made our way up to the register to pay. And I know many of you will find this hard to believe—but we did! We bought the cargo pants! What propelled us to do so was an unfortunate combination of two things: shock and pride. Shock because we could understand paying that much for a coat, or handbag, suit trousers, or for a really nice dress—but for a pair of casual cargo pants? And pride because we did not have it in ourselves to walk away and say that they were outside our budget.

My prudent friend Juliana joked with me later that day that no amount of pride would have propelled her to waste $610 on a pair of cargo pants and that we must have been mad. I agree—we became temporarily mad due to our pride! Our pride hijacked our sense and threw it out of the window!

While buying those trousers did not bankrupt us, it taught us an important lesson on pride and the new materialism. We were able to laugh about it later (I told my husband he needed to wear them every day for the rest of his life to make the purchase worth it), but at the time it was painful. So no matter what your financial state, do not let pride push you into making a purchase you do not want. If you find yourself feeling pressured by a sales assistant or if the item you are trying on is out of your price range, simply say, "No thank you, these are not for me," and move on.

The Home

There is a famous saying: "Happiness is not having what you want but wanting what you have." This is helpful to remember when rejecting the new materialism considering matters of the home.

I am not suggesting that you do not do renovations, fix up your home, or buy new furniture. But I am suggesting you do not become obsessed with it. Do you really need to spend $50,000 getting a state-of-the-art kitchen? If you have the money to do so, you love to cook, and you feel it will significantly raise the value of your property—go for it! But if you would go into debt or be quite tight for a long time because of it, it isn't necessary.

And while the thought of only having one bathroom for the entire household to share might give you the willies, Famille Chic lived happily with one bathroom. They were content with what they had. So if there are aspects to your home that are less than desirable (a bathroom that needs renovation, hand-me-down furniture, or an outdated TV), find a way to live with them or plan responsibly to update them in the future, without going out of your budget and without incurring debt. Get resourceful. Use new throw pillows to adorn a less-than-desirable couch. Use large, fluffy white towels to give your outdated bathroom a spa-like feel. Learn to live with your outdated television—perhaps you shouldn't be watching so much TV in the first place! Be content with what you have and use the energy you would spend obsessing over your interiors for other pursuits.

Tips on How to Reject the New Materialism

Analyze your spending habits. Do you constantly feel dissatisfied with what you have? Are you always on the lookout for a new purchase or upgrade? Do you constantly peruse the shops—both physical and virtual? Is your life driven by your next purchase? Do you get a rush when you buy things? Do you have any debt whatsoever? Perhaps it is time to tame the shopping demon that lives on your shoulder. When you feel the need or urge to shop, distract yourself by reading a book, cooking a meal, or going for a walk. Rather than spending a Saturday afternoon at the mall, go to a museum instead. Challenge yourself not to shop for anything other than essentials for one week.

The less shopping you do, the less you will want to do it. When you spend your free time doing other things (like writing that book you've always wanted to write), shopping may begin to seem like a waste of time. I'm not saying that you will never again find pleasure in shopping. Taking off a Wednesday afternoon to have a spot of lunch with girlfriends and a little shopping afterward will be a pleasurable treat, but shopping will no longer consume your life.

Take a cue from Famille Chic and take pleasure in what you already have. By doing so, you will flourish and prosper. Your bank account will thank you . . . and you will cultivate and maintain the vital and life-sustaining feeling of fulfillment.

Le Recap

- Avoid impulse purchases by carrying a list and only paying in cash when doing the daily shopping.

- Employ and maintain a capsule wardrobe to avoid buying too many clothes.

- Never let a salesperson sway you into purchasing something. Stand firm and don't let your pride get in the way of intelligent decision making.

- Learn to appreciate what you already have.

- Pause before making any major purchases. Wait a few days and see if you still really want them.

- Only upgrade your home if you can afford to do so.

- Analyze your spending habits and take pleasure in what you already have.

Chapter 17

CULTIVATE YOUR MIND

ntelligence is highly revered in France. People want to hear what you have to say—and what you have to say will preferably be relevant, interesting, and witty. Living and studying in Paris, I found myself, for the first time in my life, separated from all my favorite television shows, addictive gossip magazines, and other mind-numbing forms of entertainment. I found myself instead passing my time in museums, reading books, and discussing life with my fellow expats. I had never attended more cultural events in my life. It felt like a detox for my mind. It was exhilarating.

My fellow students experienced the same exhilaration. We were so busy going places, learning things, and experiencing life, we found that our new lifestyle affected our conversation. Rather than sitting together and gossiping about celebrities or who got booted off the latest reality TV show, we actually had topics of substance to discuss.

I began to realize that our intellectual renaissance wasn't due only to the fact that we were students. We had been students back home in California as well, but back home we had all the temptations that television, gossip magazines, and vapid pop songs had to offer. I began to see that our intellectual adventures were the result of our immersion into French culture. Theirs is not a celebrity-obsessed, consumer-driven culture where mindlessness is prevalent and revered. You would never see Madame Chic, for example, lounging around in an armchair watching *Keeping Up with the Kardashians* and mindlessly thumbing through *Us Weekly*. I don't think I ever saw her watching TV, and she certainly didn't read any gossip magazines.

Making oneself attractive helps in life, but generally, being a pretty face is just not enough to get you by in France. In fact, women who aren't technically beauties but who are intellectually stimulating are highly regarded and are considered to be more attractive than those who are, say, not.

Whereas in America you run the risk of being called "pretentious" for discussing intellectual or artistic pursuits like philosophy, classical music, or poetry, in France one is expected to be well versed in such subjects. I am reminded of the discussions at Madame Bohemienne's many dinner parties. Her guests were likely to ask you what book you were reading before they asked you where you were from.

When I returned to America, I found it challenging to maintain the active intellectual life I enjoyed in France. Here there is temptation around every corner. But as with most things, it is important to be aware of your weaknesses and to amend them accordingly.

Here are some tips and inspirations for cultivating your mind.

Read Books

Read as much as you can. I try to read one to two books a week. Reading keeps your brain nimble, keeps your vocabulary (not to mention your imagination) sharp, and is much more rewarding than watching television (more on that later). The more you read, the more you want to read. Perhaps you were a big reader when you were younger and now you only pull out a book if you are going to the beach. Consider dusting off your bookshelf and getting back into it.

If you find you don't have the time to read during the day, fear not, there are many other options. Audiobooks are wonderful and can make normally dreaded tasks more enjoyable. Play them while commuting, cleaning the house, or exercising. I have a penchant for vintage mysteries and keep a handful of Agatha Christie audiobooks in my car. Most days I prefer listening to audiobooks over music while I drive, and they can make a long car ride go much faster. Just make sure you do not unconsciously press on the pedal while listening to a particularly suspenseful part!

Another way to sneak reading into your day is to keep your book in your purse. Pull the book out and read it when in the waiting room at the dentist, while getting a pedicure, or while waiting for your takeout order at the local curry house. During these sometimes long waits we usually pick up a magazine and rifle through the pages or click mindlessly on our BlackBerries to pass the time. I have a Kindle and like to bring it with me everywhere I go for this very reason. An e-book reader is handy to carry along with you. I read books on mine at the hairdresser's, while waiting for my lunch (if I am alone), before getting a massage—wherever I can sneak a read in! (Lately everywhere I go, I see people reading on these devices. One day we will all wonder what we did without them!) I also like to read before I go to sleep. There is something so cozy about lying in bed with a good book . . .

For social purposes it is a good idea to keep a list in your head of interesting books you've read so the next time someone asks you if you've "read anything good lately," you'll have something to say. Add a few books you wouldn't normally read to your reading list. A book of poetry, for example, or a book on philosophy. Cultivate your mind through reading and you will be a most intriguing dinner guest at the next soirée.

Read Newspapers

We receive the *Financial Times* and the *Los Angeles Times* (weekend edition). I love having a paper delivered. Not only does it contain the news, but it also has scores of other thought-provoking articles that I never would have read if I just looked online for my news. Also, reading the news online can lead you down a slippery path. You might start out intending to read the headlines on CNN.com, but then find yourself on PopSugar reading about a teen heartthrob's latest breakup, and then an hour has passed and you are no more informed than when you started.

Watch Films

Trade in a few Hollywood blockbusters for independent and foreign films. I have developed a very low tolerance for most mainstream commercial blockbusters. Time is so precious, I would rather not waste it sitting in front of violent explosions for two and a half hours. When I go to the movies, I like to see an independent film with an interesting story to tell. Read your local paper for reviews or check out what the critics are saying online. If you have an independent movie theatre near you, write down some of the names of the upcoming films to remind yourself of what you would like to see in the future.

Also don't forget the classics. Mail-order DVD companies have an impressive array of films that can be streamed instantly or delivered to your home. I like to watch a classic film from the golden age of Hollywood at least once a month. Hitchcock is my favorite.

Follow the Arts

Keep au courant with your local museum's latest art exhibitions. Attend the theatre, ballet, and opera. Frequent concerts. Acquaint yourself with a genre of music you are unfamiliar with. If you like classical music, for example, get specific and familiarize yourself with nocturnes. Or pick up a biography of your favorite composer (mine is Chopin) so that you may better appreciate his or her work. Cultivate your artistic mind.

Improve Your Vocabulary

Subscribe to a word-of-the-day blog on the Internet. The word of the day is on my home page so that it is the first thing I see every morning when I open my computer. It expands my vocabulary and also prevents me from saying *like* too much (a terrible vice of mine, having grown up in Southern California).

Incorporate the new words you learn into your everyday speech. If someone calls you pretentious, simply give the person a Mona Lisa smile and move on with your day. Don't feel pressured into contributing to the dumbing down of society because you fear being called or thought of as pretentious. Don't even give your accuser the time of day. You don't need to associate with that type of person anyway.

Watch Less Television

The less you watch it, the less you want to watch it. In France I probably watched four hours of TV in six months. I didn't miss it in the slightest. Everyday life was just too exciting. But when I got back to America, I fell into the trap of watching it again—lots of it. For a few years I watched a couple of hours of television a day! It didn't feel right. I wasn't feeling fulfilled. I was definitely not reading as much as I liked to. I had cabin fever a lot more and overall just felt like a couch potato—not a nice feeling.

I decided to go on a "television diet," and now I watch probably a couple of hours of television a week, which feels right for me. Don't get me wrong, I still have my favorite shows (which shall remain nameless here as they are simply too embarrassing to reveal), but the difference now is that I have one or two guilty-pleasure TV shows rather than six, and I enjoy those few shows more. Now I spend more and more of my free time reading, writing, or going for walks, and I am much happier.

If you find it difficult to cut down on TV, consider rearranging the furniture in your living room to promote conversation rather than television watching. If all the seats in your living room are arranged for optimal television viewing, switch it up a little. Allow the fireplace or a work of art to be the main focal point. Make your TV a supporting character in your living room, not the main star. Hopefully this will inspire you to be more social and engage in conversations with your family or with guests rather than retreat to the hermetic comfort that chronic TV watching provides.

Travel

Travel as much as you can. Seeing other cultures is the best way to cultivate your mind and expand your horizons. (After all, look what visiting Paris did for me!) When you travel, don't just go for all the major tourist destinations. Try to immerse yourself in the culture like a native. Make some local friends. Find out-of-the-way eateries. Learn about the local writers and artists.

Also, it would be prudent to learn the customs of the country you're visiting so as to avoid committing faux pas. Of course this is not always possible . . .

One morning in Paris I awoke with an awful cold. I felt terrible, had the shivers, and definitely felt feverish. I skipped class and stayed in bed. Madame Chic was very kind and attentive and brought me hot water with lemon and a bowl of consommé. She was worried about my fever, so she also brought in a thermometer for me to take my temperature with. I thanked her and placed the thermometer in my mouth. The moment I did so, a look of horror came over Madame Chic's face. She started waving her hands uncontrollably and found herself to be quite speechless—wanting to say something but not being able to get it out.

"What is it?" I asked, with the thermometer still in my mouth.

"Jennifer! Non!" was all she could say. Her hands were still flailing. I had never seen Madame Chic lose her cool before. It must have been serious.

"What's wrong?" I asked. Perhaps Madame Chic wasn't feeling well either.

"That thermometer," she exclaimed, exasperated, "is not for the mouth! It is for the . . ." and here she made an apologetic gesture toward her bottom.

Needless to say, I spat the thermometer out of my mouth faster than a Parisian jetting through traffic at the Arc de Triomphe. At that point Madame Chic broke into uncontrollable laughter. I had not the inclination nor the sense of humor in that moment to be amused, myself, as I had just inserted the family rectal thermometer in my mouth, but later that day I was able to joke about it.

So please, learn from my mistake and let this humiliating experience of mine not be for naught. If you find yourself in need of a thermometer while staying in France, just remember where it goes.

Take Classes

Even though you are no longer in school full-time, you can still take classes. There is so much to learn—new languages, new instruments, new skills. It doesn't matter how old you are. You are never too old to learn. Put yourself out there. In my late teens and early twenties I was an actress who did a lot of theatre. I was part of a touring company that did Shakespeare for children, and I did independent plays where I could. I was always in an acting class during my acting days because it kept my craft sharp. Then in my late twenties I felt a yearning to start writing. As a child I had always wanted to be a writer when I grew up, but for one reason or another I never took a creative writing class. Feeling very nervous, I finally signed up at the L.A. Writers Lab to take a class called The 90-Day Novel. Walking into the class, I felt intimidated. I was sure I'd be surrounded by professional writers or at the least people with a lot more experience than me. Who did I think I was kidding? I almost turned back. But something kept me there (the fact that I had prepaid for my three-month session probably had something to do with it). Taking that class was one of the best decisions I have ever made in my life. Not only did it teach me a few things and give me the discipline to write every day, but it also allowed me to be a part of a community of writers who are still my friends. Without it, this book would never have been written!

Push yourself. It can be scary to take part in something new, but taking a class can really shake up things in an otherwise complacent life. Here are some ideas for classes that will add interest to your life: screenwriting, playwriting, creative writing, acting, improvisation, painting, piano, cooking, film appreciation, art appreciation, wine tasting and connoisseurship, karate, chi gong, horseback riding, French lessons. The list goes on . . .

Le Recap

- Never let yourself go intellectually. Challenge your little gray cells on a daily basis.

- Read or listen to audiobooks as much as you can.

- Seek out independent and foreign films as refreshing alternatives to the typical Hollywood blockbusters.

- Subscribe to a newspaper for their special articles and reviews.

- Be a patron of the arts in whatever field interests you most.

- Expand your vocabulary and subscribe to a word-of-the-day blog. Try to use the new words in your everyday speech.

- Watch less television. The less you watch it, the less you miss it.

- Travel as much as you can. Visit places that are out of your comfort zone (though not too far out of your comfort zone—one must be safe!) and learn about new cultures.

- No matter how old you are, take classes in whatever field interests you. Push yourself: it could just change your life.

Chapter 18

FIND SIMPLE PLEASURES

At the beginning of the film *Amélie*, the narrator introduces the characters by noting the simple pleasures that they enjoy every day. Amélie enjoys plunging her hands into the sack of grain at the market, skipping stones at the Canal Saint-Martin, and breaking the top of the crème brûlée with her spoon. Her father loves cleaning out his tool box and stripping wallpaper. Her mother's tiny pleasures are cleaning out her handbag and scrubbing the floor with her slippers. While the characters' likes are slightly eccentric and whimsical, they also showcase how the French take pleasure from the simplest things in life.

Like the characters in *Amélie*, Famille Chic took pleasure in the smallest of things. Madame Chic enjoyed listening to the morning radio show as she prepared breakfast. She loved arranging the strawberries in a symmetrical fashion on her *tarte aux fraises*. She looked forward to the morning phone call to her girlfriend in which they discussed the latest news around town. Monsieur Chic loved his pipe, his nightly slice of Camembert—the *roi du fromage*. And for vacations? Their summer house in Brittany provided endless pleasure.

Famille Chic's pleasures were simple, but they were also repetitive. They somehow found a way to enjoy the repetition of the seemingly mundane aspects of their daily life. Madame Chic's attitude could easily have been, *Here I go again, preparing breakfast for the family. Every day the same thing!* Or Monsieur Chic could have thought, *Camembert again for the cheese course? Where is the variety?* But they didn't have negative attitudes toward these repetitive details of their daily lives, and as a result, they got along very harmoniously as a family.

Extracting pleasure from simple things can be the key to a happy life. If you slow down and take pleasure in simple things, you are more likely to lead a contented and well-balanced existence and less likely to incur unhealthy habits like overspending, hoarding, and overeating. You are also more likely to be present in the moment and pleasant with your family.

Of course, having a positive attitude is important (I am reminded of my good friend Romi, who has a positively cheerful disposition no matter what the circumstance). But I'm talking about taking a step beyond positivity. Enjoying simple pleasures is about getting a kick out of life. It's about living fully in the moment and not missing a thing. It's about having a sense of humor, a sense of victory, an openness and readiness for whatever life throws at you. Maybe you enjoy a trip to the farmer's market and the sweet clementines you discovered while there. Or maybe you savor the moment you are standing next to a handsome man in an elevator; you close your eyes while inhaling the scent of his cologne. Maybe you find yourself walking by a sumptuous pink rose and stopping to admire it (and yes, even to smell it) without worrying about looking like a nutcase.

On Sisyphean Tasks

Sure, it is easy to take pleasure in agreeable things like eating tarts and smelling roses, but what about unpleasant things? What about those everyday chores that are less than fun? And what about the fact that those chores have to be repeated? How do we avoid being Sisyphus in our own lives?

You remember Sisyphus, the mythical king who was punished for all eternity by having to roll a boulder up a hill, only to watch it roll right back down again. When I studied Latin in high school, I felt extremely sorry for poor old Sisyphus. I was reminded of this mythical character while reading Alexander

McCall Smith's *The Lost Art of Gratitude*. In it, Isabel, the main character, argues that we are all Sisyphus to some extent. We clean the kitchen at night only to find it dirtied the next morning after breakfast. We file away papers at work, only to have the stack grow again by the end of the day.

My own Sisyphean plight involves such things as emptying the dishwasher, doing the laundry, and filing in the office. These rather mundane tasks always seem to be completed and then, lo and behold, all too quickly after completion need to be tackled again.

I believe the key is to enjoy the journey and appreciate the cyclical nature of the task at hand. Examine what small pleasures you can extract from unloading the dishwasher, doing laundry, or filing. Some may call this "looking on the bright side." Perhaps when you unload the dishwasher, it is early in the morning before the whole household is up. You can relish the experience of being alone, not having to take care of the needs and wants of children or spouse. Sure, you're bending down, picking up glasses, and putting them away, but look for the pleasure in the moment. Perhaps the sun is rising and the light is filtering through the window. A pot of tea is brewing and filling the kitchen with a welcome aroma. Maybe the dog has sleepily sauntered downstairs to keep you company. You get the idea.

Madame Chic really delighted in her daily repetitive tasks. She got up quite early every morning to have breakfast ready for the family. Monsieur Chic would leave the house early to go to work, so most days Madame Chic was up at 5:30 a.m.! Yet she went to the kitchen in her nice dressing gown and slippers, turned on the morning radio show, percolated the coffee, got her own tea ready, placed her homemade preserves on the table, and chatted with her husband while they had breakfast. By the time I got up (a considerable amount of time later), she was dressed and ready for the day. She never complained about getting up so early to get breakfast ready. I think she took genuine pleasure in her routine. When you learn to take pleasure in mundane tasks, the never-ending repetition of these tasks becomes less daunting.

Perhaps one of your more loathed repetitive tasks is to go to the grocery store. You feel as though you are always at the blooming grocery store! I am reminded again of Amélie, who has such a great time at the market because she looks forward to plunging her hands into the sack of grains. Could you find a similar (and perhaps more hygienic) thrill? You might take pleasure in smelling the strawberries to see which ones are the sweetest, or perusing the selection of European cheeses offered in the dairy case. Why not turn that inevitable trip into a delightful one?

The truth of the matter is, these mundane tasks must be done. There is no getting around them. Almost everyone has to do a task on a daily basis that is less than fun. The key is to find pleasure in the task and to not wish you were doing something else while doing it.

JENNIFER L. SCOTT

Employ Your Senses

When I lived in Paris, I took a wine-tasting class. I figured wine tasting was a good skill to have. I didn't want to appear naïve or gauche if asked to try a wine when dining in a restaurant. I wanted to be able to differentiate the good stuff from the bad.

When our instructor first went over the necessary steps for true wine tasting—sniffing the wine, swirling it in the glass, and finally tasting—I was a bit skeptical. Could I ever do this without coming across as pretentious? (You know how I feel about being called pretentious!) My fellow classmates and I chuckled self-consciously as we followed the instructions with our own glasses. And then, per the instructor's request, we described what we tasted: blackberries, vanilla, musk, oak—who knows what other notes we came up with. We were having good fun with the whole process, but it got me thinking. Wine tasting—the employing of the senses, the relishing of the taste, the emphasis on quality, the taking of such immense pleasure out of such a simple thing—was a metaphor for French life.

It was in Paris where I learned to taste wine properly. Appreciate perfume. Relish a three-hour dinner. Discover the nuances between different cheeses. Attentively listen to music and appreciate it. It was in Paris where my senses came alive, allowing me to extract pleasure from things I might never have paid attention to in the States.

This could have happened for several reasons. I was in college and had virtually no responsibilities to speak of. No bills to pay, no job to hold down. I was young and adventuresome with the most beautiful and romantic city in the world at my doorstep. No wonder I walked around with a perpetual spring in my step, flirting and delighting in practically everything I came across. Who could have blamed me for living such a sensory and sensual experience?

After I left Paris, however, I found myself falling into a rather bland rut. I would eat the same things all the time and not challenge my palate. I got used to the scent of my bath products and didn't really smell them anymore. I listened to vapid pop songs on the radio and zoned out on commercial breaks. I was essentially wasting the very senses that had kept me feeling so alive in Paris. It was easy to do. I wasn't in Paris anymore. Suddenly life was very different. I was graduating from college, needed to get a job, and for the first time in my life had bills to pay. There would be no more lounging around cafés and gardens exulting in life! But luckily I started to question this rather depressing turn of events and reminded myself that, as Ernest Hemingway so aptly said, Paris is a moveable feast. Why couldn't the simple pleasures I experienced while living there be found no matter where I was in the world? And no matter what my circumstances?

I learned that if you find yourself in a rut where you fail to find pleasure in the simple things in life, the best cure is to employ your senses. You do not have to be on vacation in a romantic, foreign city to live a life of rapture. You can enjoy yourself no matter what the circumstances—whether most of your day is spent working in an office or on the playground with your children. Whether you are walking down a cobblestone street in Paris or dodging pedestrians in New York. You are in control of every experience in your life. It is up to you to decide how each will go.

For example, perhaps Monday mornings are particularly cruel to you. You always have so much fun on the weekends, and then that alarm sounds and you know the start of the workweek is at hand. Oh, how tiresome! You normally (begrudgingly) get out of bed, take a quick shower, take twenty minutes to decide what on earth to wear, make your way to the kitchen, scarf down a bowl of cereal and a cup of instant coffee, and rush out the door for work. Your morning routine is so ingrained, it comes as second nature to you. You just go through the motions and somehow end up at your desk an hour later.

But could this loathed morning routine actually become pleasurable? Could it be possible that you will look forward to Monday mornings (or any morning for that matter!) one day? What if you were to shake up your morning routine by employing your senses? Put on your cashmere cardigan and appreciate the velvety soft texture on your skin. Place a dab of perfume behind your right ear so if you happen to run into a dashing stranger on your lunch break, you will entrance. Luxuriate in the aroma of your morning coffee—brewed just as you like it and with just the right amount of cream. Listen to your favorite sonata while doing all this. What a rapturous and sensuous way to get ready for the day—and why not? Pleasure should not be reserved only for traditionally pleasurable occasions.

Slow Down

Try not to rush through your day. Practice being in the moment. Do you ever have one of those days when your mind is just constantly elsewhere? Even if you are pressed for time, try to be in the present moment. There is no point in rushing from A to B. As Ralph Waldo Emerson so aptly said, "Life is a journey, not a destination." When you take the time to go through your day with mindfulness, you keep yourself open to new experiences and are therefore more readily able to delight in simple pleasures.

Don't Let Guilty Pleasures Get Out of Hand

We all have them. Guilty pleasures. Your guilty pleasures might be watching a certain soapy reality TV show, having a few chocolate truffles in the afternoon, or taking a glass of wine in the bath. If those things bring you pleasure, by all means partake! But always be mindful that you are not using your guilty pleasures as excuses to develop bad habits. Watching an entire marathon of that reality TV show, eating a whole box of chocolates instead of a few, or having one too many glasses of wine in the bath are all examples of overindulging. The whole point of pleasures is that they remain pleasurable. True pleasures do not actually induce guilt, make you feel ill, or promote unhealthy behavior.

If you feel like your guilty pleasures are getting out of hand, take a page from the characters in *Amélie* and take pleasure out of the moments in everyday life. Doing so could divert your attention from other less healthy habits. For example, if you suddenly develop a pleasurable hankering for cleaning out your handbag, like Amélie's mother, you might distract yourself from engaging in an unhealthy or addictive habit like spending another Saturday afternoon perusing the shops.

See if you can get the same kick out of cleaning your handbag or making a strawberry tart that you do from going shopping or from watching TV. Redefine what a guilty pleasure means to you. Your wallet, not to mention your soul, will thank you.

Rejoice in every aspect of life—big or small. Let nothing pass you by. Appreciate everything—whether it is perceived as good or bad. You have the power to turn any experience into a pleasurable one. Challenge your preconceptions and luxuriate in the simple things of life.

Le Recap

- Deriving pleasure from the most mundane of things can set you up for a happy and exciting life.

- Learn how to turn your Sisyphean tasks into pleasurable experiences.

- Adopting a positive outlook on life (no matter what) is key—as is a sense of humor.

- Employ your senses to derive maximum pleasure from your experiences.

- Slow down and try not to rush through your day. Make a concerted effort, and eventually, being in the present moment will come naturally to you.

Chapter 19

VALUE QUALITY ABOVE ALL

Living with Famille Chic defined for me a quality life. I also learned about things like clothing, furniture, and food, as well as quality of thoughts, of feelings, of intellect. So many things about the French lifestyle emphasize quality.

Madame Chic and her family were great role models. They sought quality in their clothes, their appearance, their décor, their food, their conversation, the time they spent together. They lived fully realized lives.

They believed they deserved to live well, and they did indeed do just that. They were genuinely content with their lives; if there were discontent, I would have known. It's terribly difficult to hide that sort of thing when living in close quarters with a family for such a long period of time.

Once you commit to living a life of quality, quality will permeate every aspect of your life. You will be more selective of the foods you choose to eat, the fabrics you choose to wear, the way you choose to spend your time. You are less likely to binge on fast food, to hastily purchase an inferior article of clothing just because it is on sale, or to sit for hours in front of the TV while your life slips away.

Famille Chic's penchant for quality things and experiences was inspiring and, as I have subsequently discovered, theirs is a way of life that is entirely within reach.

Quality Food

Eating quality food is one of the great pleasures of life. Become a connoisseur of fine food. Seek out the highest quality available. High-quality food doesn't have to be expensive! I finally decided to start frequenting the local farmer's market, which is famous the world over for its delectable offerings. I began going to the farmer's market as part of my commitment to incorporating exercise into my everyday life and because I missed the vibrant and enticing outdoor markets in Paris and the South of France.

On my first trip to the Santa Monica farmer's market I bought some heirloom tomatoes, a box of strawberries, some summer squash, and a handful of sprouts. The whole transaction was very inexpensive. Later that day I sliced one of the giant yellow heirloom tomatoes, arranged the pieces artfully on a plate, and sprinkled a small amount of sea salt on top. My husband and I tried the delicacy and were amazed at how flavorful and enticing the tomato was. We had become so accustomed to eating the anemic, flavorless varieties found in the supermarket that we had forgotten what a proper tomato should taste like! The strawberries were bursting with sweetness and required no sugar to make them edible. After indulging in a few strawberries, my husband (who is not one for superlatives) exclaimed that he hadn't tasted a berry so sweet since he'd been a young boy in England!

Once you train your palate to appreciate only the best food, you will eliminate any desire for inferior food, a change that can be quite handy if you are trying to kick your snacking habit. It does take a while, but soon you won't crave the processed, packaged, low-quality foods you may have enjoyed in the past and you will make wiser choices when ordering at restaurants. Becoming a foodie or food connoisseur is quite fun and can prove to be a fruitful hobby.

It is important to note here, however, that you shouldn't become a snob. Do your best to avoid turning up your nose at any inferior food that is served to you—whether in a restaurant or at a friend's dinner party. Always be gracious and appreciative of what food is put in front of you. After all, if you come across as a snob, it might affect your social calendar a bit.

Quality Clothing

Become a connoisseur of fabrics and craftsmanship. You may spend more on a garment than you would have in the past, but the garment will last you a long time, provided it is looked after properly.

Once you have made the transition to having a ten-item or capsule wardrobe, you will not want to put anything in your closet that isn't of the best quality you can afford. It would be the equivalent of snacking on liquor store Ding Dongs when you are accustomed to having molten chocolate cakes. Poor-quality clothing simply won't do anymore.

Be an Informed Consumer

We are lucky to be living in the age of the Internet. There is no more helpful tool for making informed decisions. What with reviews, ratings, blogs, and consumer-oriented websites, we are able to make educated choices about every purchase we make.

We can save an enormous amount of money and aggravation in the long run.

When my husband and I were preparing for the arrival of our first baby, I needed to purchase a whole slew of products I knew nothing about—cribs, bouncers, diapers, high chairs (this list really could go on and on). I knew I wanted everything to be the best quality we could afford. Rather than walking around the shops and hazarding a guess as to what would be best for our baby, we went on the Internet to read articles and reviews and were generally happy with every purchase we made. We saved a lot of money. Baby paraphernalia is expensive! We got it right the first time and avoided extra expense.

Being an informed consumer isn't just about knowing which crib is the highest rated on the baby website. It also involves ethical and environmental issues. When purchasing meat, poultry, fish, and eggs, you'll want to know where those purchases came from and how those animals were raised. The more people insist on consuming organic, free-range, and hormone-free meat and dairy products, the more these products will be readily available.

Another great way to make informed, quality decisions regarding the products you consume is to look at the company that makes them. Does the company have environmentally friendly business practices? Creating the demand for such qualities can only bring more good from companies that wish to compete for your business.

Quality Experiences

You have the power to make every experience in your life one of quality. The choice is yours. In the previous chapter we discussed taking simple pleasures from the mundane aspects of life in order to live a richer and more fulfilling existence. Taking pleasure from the small things is one tactic, but the most effective way to achieve a life of quality is to have a good attitude.

If there is anything that is causing you stress, put it into perspective by looking at it objectively. Go on a negativity diet. Eliminate any negative people from your friendship roster. Life is too precious to get bogged down in other people's drama. Of course you must be there for your friends and family when they go through difficult times—as you would hope they will be there for you—but be wary of people who are chronically going through a difficult time. Is their negativity taking a toll on your life? If you do find yourself in a negative experience, try to learn from it and see what good you can take from it.

Look at the fun and joy in any situation and always come from a place of love. Doing so will ensure that every experience you have, whether good or bad, is a quality experience.

Quality Time

When spending time with your family, always make it quality time. It might be that the only time during the day your whole family gets together is at the dinner table. If this is the case, it is especially important that this be quality time. The television is off, all phones are on silent, the computer is in sleep mode. The table is set with love, and the food is nourishing and presented with care. Talk to each other. What were the best and worst parts of the day? Laughter amongst loved ones is the best sound in the world. Create a sacred ritual of spending quality time with your family.

We are often on our best behavior with strangers and guests, but when it comes to our family, those customs fly out the window. Use your best manners with your family too. Let them know that you love them on a daily basis. Create the foundation for treating each other with respect. I was always impressed by Monsieur and Madame Chic's relationships with their five children. Their children were deeply respectful of their parents, got along very well with each other, and loved visiting home on a regular basis. This could have had a lot to do with Madame Chic's spectacular dinners, but there was more to it than that. There was a lot of laughter and love in that house. The children wanted to come back because they knew any time spent with their family would be quality time.

How I Became a Daily Connoisseur

In 2008 I started my blog, *The Daily Connoisseur,* to explore the very topics written about in this book. A daily connoisseur is someone who seeks quality in every moment of every day—

someone who is able to appreciate life to its fullest. But the seeds for becoming a daily connoisseur were planted in my mind long before the blog. It was even before living in Paris with Famille Chic . . .

As I have previously mentioned, when I was eighteen years old, I spent six weeks with my mother and father on the Côte d'Azur in the South of France. My father, who is a college professor, was working for the summer as a tutor to a privileged student of his whose family had a yacht docked in Cannes. Visiting Cannes was my first European experience, and as anyone familiar with the South of France could tell you, it is a very glamorous place to be.

Of course at eighteen one is very impressionable, and I was quite impressed by the way people lived in this wealthy little seaside town. People dressed up during the day and even more so at night. Protocol was important—table manners, street manners, the way everyone referred to me as *mademoiselle*, delightful! I began to observe customs like taking an apéritif before dinner and the joyous interlude of the afternoon espresso at the local café.

I made it my mission to observe—in cafés, walking on the Croisette, lounging by the hotel pool, lunching in seaside restaurants, doing a bit of shopping with my mother. I saw that the inhabitants of this exclusive town seemed to enjoy and relish absolutely every single moment of their lives. Life was fun!

I spent those six weeks in a state of semi-nirvana. I had only really known the small town back in California where I grew up. It was wonderful to be exposed to such a dazzling lifestyle. We took day trips to Monaco and Saint-Tropez. Yes, I was wowed by the sheer opulence of these places, but I was also intrigued by the French lifestyle. These were people who were well dressed, well groomed, well shod, and in great shape. They were people who were getting a tickle out of life. I wanted to see more. I wanted to experience more, and after my six-week holiday was over, I made immediate plans to study French at college and to somehow make my way back to France. This time, to Paris—to the capital of it all. I wanted to become a connoisseur of daily life like the people I saw—to lead a life of quality. And thus the seed was planted . . .

Le Recap

- Commit to living a life of quality to tune your mind to the concept of fine living.

- Become more selective of the foods you eat, the clothes you wear, and the way you choose to spend your time.

- Become a connoisseur of fine specialty food.

- Be an informed consumer. Before making purchases, read reviews and research companies and products.

- Make every experience you have a quality one by adopting a good attitude and sense of humor about life.

- Make the time you spend with your family and friends quality time.

Chapter 20

LIVE A PASSIONATE LIFE

learned many lessons from my time in Paris, but the most profound lesson I learned was to lead a life of passion. Every detail of life can become exceptional if you allow it to be so. You hold the key. When filled with laughter, friendship, art, intellectual endeavors, and a certain joy, life can be extraordinary. Allow yourself to be moved on a daily basis. Every day when you step out of bed, you have the choice either to go through the motions and merely exist or to go about with passion, to always be present in your own life, to take something from every situation—whether it is good or bad.

While I was living in Paris, every aspect of my life was infused with passion. I became ready for all the pleasures that life had to offer. I got the biggest kicks out of the simplest things—listening to Chopin on the record player after a satisfying dinner chez Famille Chic, having a delectable slice of Madame Bohemienne's flourless chocolate cake, reading a particularly well written verse of poetry while sunning in the Jardin des Tuileries . . . In Paris I lived an intensely satisfying existence. Life was a passionate affair.

Of course, it didn't start out that way. I started my sojourn in France wanting to be constantly in control. I was so far away from my family—from my beloved Southern California with all its casual comforts. To begin with, I was shy and rarely ventured from my routine haunts: Madame Bohemienne's, my classes at the Sorbonne and at the American University, and of course, Famille Chic's Sixteenth Arrondissement abode. Of course I ventured out in the city, but I was always with my closest friends, map firmly in hand.

But eventually, after I started to get the hang of my surroundings and became fairly fluent in the language, I began to breathe the breath of the city. I started to let go a bit. I would often venture off alone and spend an afternoon at the Musée d'Orsay or walking on the Champs-Élysées. I would sit in cafés all by myself, comforted by the fact that I knew no one around me and could devour the daily dramas that would take place before me on the Parisian boulevard. I started to feel like a true Parisian.

One night about a month into my stay I was invited to go to a nightclub with some new friends I had made. I hadn't been out late at night thus far because I didn't want to give Madame Chic the impression that I was a party animal. But I figured it was time. Wearing a shimmery gold tank top, black tuxedo trousers, and high heels, I took the metro to the center of Paris to meet up with my friends for a late-night supper. Afterward we made our way to the nightclub Les Bains.

Giddy from champagne (we splashed out a bit at dinner), we entered the nightclub. It was heaving with Parisians, and it seemed like everyone in the room was dancing. I made my way to one of the platforms so I could look at all the revelers while I danced. I danced for three hours straight in a complete state of euphoria. That night, life coursed through my veins. It was one of the most memorable nights of my life because it was one of the first times I truly let go.

That night any worries I had were thrown away. Small worries such as would I make the last metro to Famille Chic's home? (I didn't.) Or would I pass the requisite French grammar exam at the end of the semester? (I did.) And also big worries like what would I do when I left Paris? What direction would life take me? Could I ever capture this happiness again?

As my life evolves, those questions are still being answered. Now that I am older, with a husband and daughters, I find myself the Madame Chic of my own family. I learned so much from her and from living in Paris, I want to share this wealth of knowledge with my daughters. The one thing I want for both of them is that they live lives of passion. It doesn't matter what they do—the important thing is *how* they do it. I hope they will be present and ready for whatever this funny life has in store for them.

Eckhart Tolle, the new age philosopher, says, "What you do is secondary. How you do it is primary." Now, while Eckhart Tolle isn't French, his philosophy here is. It is important to do what you are passionate about, but if you find yourself doing something mundane, do it passionately.

My hope for everyone who reads this book is that you are able to lead a passionate life—one filled with love, art, and music. One that you will be able to reflect back on and say that you lived well—that no moment was wasted.

It is easy to coast through life on autopilot and barely feel a thing. So many of us do it . . . wandering through our lives relatively unconscious. Not using our senses, not feeling, not *living*.

That first day in Paris, standing on the doorstep of Famille Chic's home, I had no idea what journey I was about to embark on. I was about to go on the biggest adventure I'd ever known. Thrust into a strange and beautiful land. Living with a formal family like one out of an old-fashioned novel—with their decadent meals, their beautiful apartment, that inspiring space.

Making friends with Madame Bohemienne and her artistic companions—those passionate, wine-fueled gatherings.

Walking across the beautiful city in the icy cold. Feeling so completely content as a solitary figure riding the metro on the way to school or walking down the Champs-Élysées looking at all the chic people.

Being so grateful when a moment could be shared with someone else. Those bursts of feeling that came upon me when I saw the secret midnight quartet at the Louvre. When I saw my first Manet at the Musée d'Orsay. Every night having a slice of Camembert—the *roi du fromage.*

Every now and then I close my eyes and remember the first time I stood on the doorstep of Famille Chic, butterflies in my stomach, going mad with the amazing possibility of life.

And then, I step across the threshold . . .

Resources

Beauty Products

Arbordoun www.arbordoun.com

Benedetta www.benedetta.com

Brazilian Peel www.brazilianpeel.com

Clarisonic www.sephora.com

Claus Porto www.clausporto.com

Dermalogica www.dermalogica.com

Diptyque www.diptyqueparis.com

Éminence www.eminenceorganics.com

Epicuren www.epicuren.com

L'Occitane www.loccitane.com

Paula's Choice www.paulaschoice.com

Roger & Gallet www.roger-gallet.com

Sibu Beauty www.sibubeauty.com

Skindinävia www.skindinavia.com

Books

Sixty Million Frenchmen Can't be Wrong by Jean-Benoît Nadeau and Julie Barlow (Sourcebooks, 2003)

The 90-Day Novel by Alan Watt (The 90-Day Novel Press, 2010)

The Lost Art of Gratitude by Alexander McCall Smith (Anchor, 2010)

Fashion

A.P.C. www.apc.fr

BCBG Max Azria www.bcbg.com

Diane von Furstenberg www.dvf.com

Ferragamo www.ferragamo.com

James Perse www.jamesperse.com

J Brand www.jbrandjeans.com

J. Crew www.jcrew.com

London Sole www.londonsole.com

Nanette Lepore www.nanettelepore.com

Rebecca Taylor www.rebeccataylor.com

Velvet www.velvet-tees.com

Vince www.vince.com

Films

Amélie by Jean-Pierre Jeunet

Je ne dis pas non by Iliana Lolitch

Si c'était lui . . . by Anne-Marie Etienne

Shall We Kiss? by Emmanuel Mouret

Music

Yo-Yo Ma: *La Voix du Violoncelle*

The San Francisco Saxophone Quartet: *Tails of the City*

Sidney Bechet: *Petite Fleur*

French Dinner Party: iTunes Essentials compilation

Services

Petite Spa: www.petitespa.net

Madeline Poole Nails: http://madelinepoolenails.tumblr.com

Acknowledgments

Writing this book has been an incredible journey and I have many people to thank who helped me along the way: my mother and father for nurturing my interests and sending me to Paris—I appreciate it more than you could ever know; my darling husband, Ben, for just being the best; my wonderful agent, Erica Silverman, and everyone at Trident Media Group; my marvelous editor, Trish Todd, and the team at Simon & Schuster for believing in the book; Virginia Johnson for your delightful illustrations; my sister, Leslie Kahle, for your beautiful artwork on the original book; my cousin Kristy Evans without whom life would be very dull indeed (Remember our three-hour dinner in front of the Eiffel Tower?); my grandmother Lila for your inspirational joie de vivre; my mother-in-law, Jane, a Madame Chic in her own right; and everyone in my family, both in America and England, for your love and support.

Deepest gratitude to: Juliana Patel, Romi Dames, Meg De-Loatch, Lilliam Rivera, Liesl Schillinger, Jennifer Seifert, Anjali Rajamahendran, Keely Deller, Danya Solomon, Rich Evans, Bryan Evans, Matt Weinstein, Chan Phung, Annasivia Britt, Newton Kaneshiro, Kelly Foster, Nancy Bush, Jennifer Durrant, Amelia Deboree, Bex Hartman, Jennifer Bates, Brian Peterson, Jacqueline DeArmond, Maggie Katreva, Maria Caamal, Dax Bauser, and, of course, Gatsby.

Thank you to my writing teacher and mentor, Alan Watt. Taking your class at the L.A. Writers Lab changed my life. *Merci* to Famille Chic, Famille Bohemienne, and the city of Paris for providing me with so much inspiration. And, very important, thank you to all the readers of *The Daily Connoisseur*. Your encouragement and support inspired me to write this book. Without you it would not exist. And finally, thank you to my beautiful daughters, Arabella and Georgina. You are my raison d'être. I love you.

About the Author

Jennifer L. Scott is the writer and editor of *The Daily Connoisseur* (www.dailyconnoisseur.com). She lives in Santa Monica, California, with her eccentric husband, adorable daughters, and distinguished Chihuahua. *Lessons from Madame Chic: 20 Stylish Secrets I Learned While Living in Paris* is her first book.

Learn more at www.jenniferlscott.com.